AN UNFASHIONABLE CANCER

FROM RUNNING A FASHION BUSINESS
TO WAKING UP WITH KIDNEY CANCER
AN ADVENTURE FROM FASHION VICTIM
TO CANCER SURVIVOR

BY DEBBIE MURPHY

This book is a journal, taken from the author's own notes and represents the authors recollections of experiences over time.
Although each of the chapters of this book remain factual, some names have been changed or omitted to protect the identity of the individual or location.
Any perceived slight of any individual or organisation is purely unintentional
ISBN 9798719802121
Cover design by Justin Robert Price
Printed in the United Kingdom

I Dedicate this Book to
My Family for your unconditional love and constant support.
Our NHS to whom I will be forever grateful.
To everyone who has worn a hospital gown.
My story would have remained a series of scribbled notes were it not for the encouragement of fellow patients who recognised themselves in my words.
Thank you for giving me the confidence to continue writing.

Contents

INTRODUCTION

empathy
[ˈɛmpəθi]
NOUN
the ability to understand and share the feelings of another.

My cancer story is not typical. Despite rising up the cancer league tables; kidney cancer is still not widely known about. Like many other parts of the body infected with this disease instead of specialist units, patients are placed on the most applicable hospital wards, in my case renal.

I arrived via blue light to an emergency department backed up with trolleys. I was whisked away to another hospital where the ward staff had more patients than beds. I encountered nurses who had lost their patience with patients ringing buzzers. Doctors with no time for small talk who delivered life shattering news without making eye contact.

Amidst this there were angels, staff who went above and beyond their duties despite lack of time and ongoing fatigue. The hand holders, bed straighteners, joyful singers and huggers, who recognised that the human touch, can often be more vital than the prescription drug.

It was no easy decision to publicise my experience. The suggestion to write a book came from fellow patients. My reluctance stemmed from fear of casting a bad light on parts of the NHS. As well as the overwhelming gratitude I owe to the medical professionals that have cared for me, I am also a Mother to two nurses; a Sister in an Emergency Department and a District Nurse. I have seen first-hand the tireless work and dedication of nursing staff, paramedics, health care assistants, cleaners, porters, doctors and specialist consultants. They are the real frontline heroes. They are also human and like us are not infallible. In the face of continuous and rising admissions, budgetary constraints, fatigue, complaints and mismanagement they can have bad days. Unfortunately, sometimes this impacts on patient care.

The lesson I've learned is to speak up more. I should have pressed the buzzer when I needed it and I regret not pushing for answers. Dressed in a hospital gown, in pain and alone it is easier to nod and accept. Those gowns strip away our identities and remove confidence. Faced with life changing diagnosis we can feel anonymous, known by the clipboard at the foot of a bed. The victims of time constraints. The hand we need to hold, the giver of explanations has another twenty-five patients to see before their management meeting.

For the most part my care was exemplary. The NHS saved my life. Where care was poor it was never personal. These are systemic failures that build and manifest into individual and often unavoidable error.

Medical knowledge is advancing constantly. With half of the proceeds from this book being directed to the dedicated charities that helped me, that's a little more funding towards the research and patient support we so desperately need. One of the most important practices that cannot be judged by an exam or given in a lecture is empathy. This must be systemically developed and introduced into patient care. We need the hand holders and bed straighteners, joyful singers and huggers to be the role models for the future of our health service.

This is my story. It doesn't have to be yours.

FORWARD

We all know the saying 'walk a mile in my shoes'. Here Debbie gives us that chance to view her world from the day she was rushed into Hospital, through her cancer diagnosis, treatment and beyond. Her honesty and style of writing allows us to look into the cancer abyss and experience the feelings of loss, confusion and loneliness that can invade your life just as much as the cancer itself. Debbie's writing gives us an insight into the strengths and weaknesses of the National Health Service which, in the UK, is the safety net that provides the vital infrastructure of clinicians, hospitals and treatments without which our fall into the cancer abyss would be final and absolute.

The failures of the clunky bureaucratic NHS machine when you are alone and in pain, reduced Debbie to tears of despair, and should not be glossed over. If we want the NHS to truly put patients at the heart of everything it does, we need to acknowledge these problems and work together to put things right for patients in the future.

But Debbie's story is also about personal triumph together with her determination to seek out the best care and treatment and not allow herself to be subsumed by cancer. The stories of kindness, empathy and compassion from some of the people she met along this bumpy road, together with the unerring love and support of her family, have bought her to where she is today. She is our Debbie, a fashion designer, a wife and mother, a businesswoman, a sportswoman, who also happens to be a kidney cancer patient.

My hope is that Debbie's open and honest account of her 'journey' with kidney cancer will inspire other cancer patients to share their experiences, become informed patients and advocate for the best possible care and treatment. One in two people will experience cancer in their lifetime, we must get better at looking after people emotionally as well as physically.

Rose Woodward
Fellow Kidney Cancer Survivor - Founder of the Kidney Cancer Support Network
www.kcsn.org.uk

PART ONE A RUDE AWAKENING

CHAPTER 1 WARDROBE MALFUNCTIONS

I lay with my eyes closed for a while listening to the rain falling steadily. The smell of coffee from my bedside table told me that Jay was awake and then I remembered, it's photoshoot day!

Pushing myself up onto my elbows I squinted at the alarm clock, 6 something. Swinging my legs out of the bed caused a sudden head-rush and I flopped back down, reaching for my new glasses. First pair of varifocals, is that an age thing? Forty-six this year, or am I forty-five? Definitely an age thing! 6.15am I need a wee.

Something isn't right, I feel a bit lightheaded but not in a 'just woken up' kind of way and I'm cold. I hold the wall as I walk across the landing, mustn't have slept well last night I'm tired. Then I'm sitting on the loo waiting, waiting and nothing, I can't wee. It's not that I don't need to I just can't but then when I look down there's blood. What the hell's that?!

Climbing back into bed I turn to Jay. "I don't think I'm very well." I felt tears stinging my eyes as I told him what had happened, and I couldn't understand why. Outside the rain dripped steadily onto the sill and it still felt more night than day.

"Do you think you need to see a doctor?"

"I'll see once I'm up and about." I wiped my tears and took my phone from the bedside table. "Sounds like my photoshoot's rained off today, I'd best message Sam." Changing the subject helped me get myself together. *What's wrong with me?* The coffee helped wake my senses as I text.

'Rain stops play and I don't feel too good, we're going to have to sort another day for the photos sorry, I'll let Shiraz know xxx.'

Sam was a three kiss texter, not one of those who vary so you're never sure what the text/kiss protocol is. Sam was reliable and hardworking; she'd written to me for work experience the previous year straight from fashion college and was incredibly talented but not confident. I'd encouraged her to go her own way, but we'd somehow ended up working together often and sharing photoshoots, well would have been.

Scrolling through my contacts I stopped at 'Shiraz Model' and typed. 'Hi, I'm really sorry for the late notice but I'm calling the shoot off, this rain looks like it's on for the day. Let me know when you're next free and we'll sort another date.' One kiss or two? I checked his last text, two. I hated letting people down, I felt bad.

6.30am Jay was getting ready for work so I pulled my dressing gown around me and headed downstairs to make another drink. I took it steady; my head still feeling other worldly. From the kitchen I stared out at the grey sky, the rain fell steadily and the wind was picking up, a typical March day dawned. Another hour and Ruby would be on her way home, our youngest daughter was working a night shift at the District

Hospital. She'd recently qualified as a staff nurse and got a job on a ward in the same hospital as her sister. Our eldest daughter, Joey had been working as a nurse in the emergency department for three years and loved her job so much she'd inspired her sibling to join the profession.

As the kettle boiled, I turned to make my drink, that's when it hit. The most agonising pain I had ever felt. It was excruciating and struck me like a knife straight through my back in the left side. I grabbed the sink, but I was sliding down as if a weight was dragging me to the floor.

Our two dogs Spider and Finn had, until then been curled up in their baskets but were now stood over me. Spider, a border collie was nosing me gently, Finn the terrier and still a pup thought it must be some kind of game, darting from one side to the other.

I needed to shout Jay upstairs but from my position on the kitchen floor he probably wouldn't hear. Slowly and painfully, I began dragging myself across the cold stone floor. I loved our kitchen for its size but right now it seemed a huge distance to cross. Inch by inch I pulled myself along accompanied by two curious dogs until I reached the stair gate, put up to stop Finn bolting through the house. Reaching to unfasten it sent more lightning flashes of pain down my side as I crossed into the living room. Laminate was at least easier to slide across and marginally warmer. When I was almost at the door to the hallway, I shouted Jay and heard him come to the top of the stairs.

"You ok?" As he began descending the stairs my tears came again. "What's happened?" Jay was soon kneeling at my side.

"I don't know. Pain." I held my left side, even talking hurt.

"Ok, well can you get up?" Jay had never seen me like this, completely helpless. "How did it start?"

"Just now, pain down my back." I attempted to take his arm and lift myself to the settee but the stabbing in my side sent me back to the floor.

"I think you need to go to hospital?" Jay was questioning, this was a new experience for us both. The only other time I'd been in hospital was to give birth apart from a couple of minor outpatient appointments. Neither of us had ever experienced anything serious enough to warrant hospital care. Was this a hospital case? It's weird the multitude of questions that went through my head in those microseconds. *I hurt bad. I've got work. Is this serious? Will they send me away? Am I wasting their time? Will it ease off?*

"Shall I phone an ambulance?" This question brought me to my senses.

"No, just drive me to the local hospital". Our nearest hospital had a minor injuries unit and was a pit stop for people in the town before heading to one of the bigger hospitals a little further away. I'd taken Joey our eldest frequently as a baby when she developed asthma until it became so bad, we would head straight to the District Hospital a short drive away via ambulance. Again, this information was being processed in my head. Go to the local hospital, it'll probably be fine, if it isn't they'll send me to the District, their decision. Making any decision right now was difficult.

"Ok, well I'll have to get you up somehow, let me grab my things first."

As Jay got up to get his shoes on, I asked. "Can you get me some trousers, and a jacket?" He looked down on me frowning.

"You need to get to hospital; they won't care what you're wearing."

"No but I do, I can't go in my pyjamas."

Jay sighed and as he turned to climb the stairs asked, "What trousers do you want?"

"Bottom drawer, Gwen Stefani pull on ones." The designer trousers I'd bought were the only ones I could think of that had an elasticated waist. Most of my wardrobe wasn't practical in the slightest. I certainly couldn't slide my way into skinny jeans and I wasn't a tracky bottoms kind of girl, I possessed nothing sensible. I listened as drawers were opened and closed and then Jay bounded back down the stairs holding the trousers and a fleece jacket.

I lay like a rag doll as Jay gently pulled my pyjamas bottoms off and began feeding my legs into the Gwen Stefani's. They may have been elasticated but what I hadn't bargained for was the lining, they had mesh inside and silky outer fabric. This meant Jay had to almost jiggle me into them which wasn't helped by the laminate floor. As he tried pulling them up, I slid around the living room yelping in pain. The cost of fashion carries a price, in this case a bloody painful one. It was one of those moments where you think, we'll laugh about this one day...

Note to self; always have an emergency outfit.

Eventually the trousers were up and he was rolling me carefully into the jacket, just the small matter of getting me to the car next.

We live on a busy main road near to the town centre, no parking outside. The car was in a side road, not far but it meant walking the short distance around the corner and across the road, not possible in my state.

"I'm going to drive the car right outside the house, I'll stick the hazards on a minute it'll be ok, it'll have to be." Jay snatched his keys and was out the door. I looked back at the two dogs standing at the stair gate.

"It's ok, I'll be back soon." I lay back waiting until Jay reappeared. He checked the back door was locked, gave the dogs a couple of treats then turned his attention back to me.

"We're just going to have to do this, you'll be ok."

Bending down beside me he gently began to lift my shoulders. I can't ever remember a pain like it, but I knew it was the only way. I couldn't face an ambulance outside the house. Slowly Jay managed to manoeuvre my arm across his shoulder and lift me carefully until both feet were on the floor. From there he took my weight and virtually carried me whimpering to the car where he fed me into the seat as carefully as possible and we headed for minor injuries.

CHAPTER 2 FASHION VICTIM

The hospital was a five-minute drive but every turn and bump in the road caused the pain to intensify. Jay pulled up outside the main doors and dashed inside reappearing with a wheelchair. After easing me back out of the passenger seat and into the chair we approached the reception of the small minor injuries department. By this stage I was ready to pass out with the pain and can't remember much of what was being said. Jay had given a brief description of my symptoms to the nurse on triage duty who read through the longest, most irrelevant questionnaire before I could be assessed. I was then taken to a side room and helped up on to a bed. It was now 8.15am.

Having established what they could about my past medical history the two nurses assessing me now turned their attention to my present predicament, blood loss and acute pain. More questioning took place; I was even asked whether it could be an ectopic pregnancy. The longer they deliberated the more agitated I became; couldn't they just make the pain go away? Eventually it was decided that I should be sent via ambulance to the District Hospital as there was nothing they could do for me in minor injuries. I'd been given paracetomol, but it was having no effect.

Suddenly everything seemed very real. Whatever was happening to me wasn't going to go away. An ambulance arrived in less than five minutes giving Jay and I no time to think ahead. The paramedics transferred me onto a stretcher and wheeled me outside to the waiting vehicle. Jay walked beside holding my bag containing keys, purse, and phone which he'd grabbed on the way out of the house.

"Take my things with you," I urged, "I'll be fine, just meet me later at the District." I couldn't see why Jay needed to come along. He could be waiting hours and once I'd had decent pain killers it should get easier.

"I need to know you're ok, I should be with you." Jay held on to my hand tightly, the concern in his eyes clearly visible.

"I'll be looked after, there's nothing you can do," I reassured. "Go to work and if there's any problem they'll call you, won't they?" I turned to the paramedic now attaching an oxygen mask to me as they raised the stretcher into the ambulance. He nodded agreement.

"They're backed up at the District to be honest, there's already a two hour wait for beds. Don't worry, we won't leave your wife until they've done handover there, she won't be alone." The paramedic did his best to remove Jay's fear and reassure him. It worked and as he kissed me goodbye, he handed my bag over.

"No keep it," I insisted, I won't need anything and you'll know where I am". *If only I knew then what I know now...*

There was no time to reconsider as the ambulance doors swung shut and we headed to A&E, I don't recall realising the gravity of the situation. I can't forget the pain though and we hadn't gone far when it had increased so much I was crying out in agony. Gary the paramedic travelling in the back with me called to the driver to pull over. He decided that I'd need morphine and quickly canulated my wrist to feed the pain relief through.

"Hold on tight, we've got the blue light on so won't be long." Gary reassured me as he scanned the notes he'd been handed at the local hospital. "It says here you appear pale and distressed but otherwise fit and well," he laughed shaking his head. "Oh, and a diagnosis of anxiety! Well it's the worst case of anxiety I've ever had to treat."

Apparently, it seemed that our local hospital hadn't managed to identify the cause of my symptoms other than I appeared very worried. They weren't wrong there!

As the ambulance weaved its way through streets busy with school runs and work traffic, I began to feel some benefit from the pain relief, but not much.

"So, are you a biker then?" I couldn't believe what Gary just asked me, I thought he'd said, 'Are you a pikey then?'

"What? A pikey?!" At this Gary nearly fell off his bench laughing.

"A Biker! I'm looking at those trousers you're wearing and they look like the kind you'd see a Hells Angel in."

Now I was laughing and crying in pain at laughing. "These are Gwen Stefani designer trousers, *biker?!*"

"I think I prefer pikey now." Gary roared with laughter as his mate Steve leaned back over his seat.

"What's going on in there, everything ok?"

"We've got a designer traveller in the back," Gary joked, at the same time inspecting my cannula and checking my observations. This was turning out to be the most bizarre morning ever.

Pulling up outside the District Hospital, Steve the driver came to open the back doors, taking down the ramp outside the rear entrance. Gary meanwhile covered me over with a baby blue cellular blanket and did a final update of my notes ready for handover to the Emergency Department staff. Between them they wheeled me out and into an already bustling A&E, the time was 8.55am.

CHAPTER 3 STAGE FRIGHT

We didn't get far as trolleys were backed up along the corridor which led into the large open space containing the Emergency Department. The huge room was sectioned into two sides, Minors and Majors each of which had a line of curtained cubicles along the walls. The Triage room attached to this sorted incoming patients so that they were seen according to the degree of urgency and treatment needed. When we arrived, there were no cubicles free and neither did there appear to be any nursing staff available for the paramedics to hand over to. The scene we met didn't faze Gary or Steve who had already resigned themselves to a lengthy wait.

"We can't just leave you here." Gary explained. "There are strict guidelines about handover and until it's completed, you're still technically our patient." Steve had managed to stop a Health Care Assistant long enough to glean that the current wait time was three and a half hours. Gary, meanwhile, manoeuvred my trolley out of the main thoroughfare and up against some large cupboard doors, the only space available.

Almost immediately it was obvious this wasn't a good place to wait as my trolley was repeatedly wheeled backwards and forwards because the cupboard contained bed linen. Each time I was pushed back against the doors the jolt sent new shocks of pain through my side. My painkillers were wearing off and Gary was becoming more concerned about the deterioration in my condition. Leaving me with Steve he went to speak to the nurse in charge, returning with her she agreed I'd have to be moved as soon as possible and went to make arrangements.

Within minutes I was wheeled into a cubicle in majors. "Time for us to say goodbye." Gary and Steve helped as I was lifted over onto the hospital trolley and then they were gone. I don't remember saying goodbye as I was being hooked up to monitors and administered more painkillers.

I was left with a Health Care Assistant who had been given the task of getting a urine sample from me. "I can't wee," I repeated.

"I'm sure you can try," she coaxed.

"I really can't, I haven't been able to since I woke up, read my notes."

"I'll pop this here then; have a go and I'll be back shortly."

Was she deaf? I can't wee! She'd placed some kind of cardboard bowl on the bed next to me. I mean, how on earth was I supposed to wee in it anyway when I couldn't move for the pain?! I lay there trying to take in my surroundings. The curtains had been considerately left half open so that anyone entering majors would have a decent view of me and my wee bowl should I attempt to climb aboard. I was still dressed in the Gwen Stefani's, but my fleece had been removed so that a cannula could be inserted. I'm not sure whether my Moomin pyjama top really went with the Gwen's? My fleece and trainers had been put in a carrier bag which now sat at the end of the bed I lay upon.

Oh, here we go.

"Have you been?" The HCA reappeared.

"There's absolutely no way I can wee, it won't come out and I can't move." My tears were coming.

"I'll be back in a minute." With that she disappeared again flicking the curtain back but making sure my audience would not be disappointed should I decide to attempt a wee.

From where I lay, I could see the queue of trolleys lined up against the corridor wall; patients waiting to be seen, their friends or relatives pacing around. The humdrum of noise was constant, bleeping machines, buzzing oxygen tanks, clatter of equipment and a multitude of voices. Amongst the chatter I heard a familiar voice and my eyes scanned the trolleys. There, right outside my cubicle lay my Moms' elderly neighbour, Cyril calling for a nurse to help him. I hadn't noticed at first as he was facing the opposite way but every so often he raised his head to shout. "Nurse, NURSE!"

This wasn't good. I didn't want my Mom knowing I was in hospital; she'd be worried sick. I needed to know what was wrong before I let her or anybody else know. Now, me and my pot were completely on show to the assembled patients and Cyril was in prime position. Every time he raised himself to call, I'd attempt to rotate my head so that he wouldn't recognise me, it was absolute agony.

Cyril lay prostrate but frequently lifted his head and shoulders to call again. Each time this happened I would struggle to twist myself around and curse under my breath, it was ridiculous.

The curtains flew back and there she was again, "Any good?" The HCA picked up my bowl and shook her head.

"Shut the curtain," I whispered.

"We have to keep the curtain open in case you take a turn for the worse."

Could it possibly get any worse?

"I'll try and get the doctor to see you now" she offered and out she went again, stopping to speak to Cyril on the way past. Not long after he was pushed out of my view and I could at least drop my guard for a while.

No doctor arrived but a porter came in and explained he'd been sent to take me up for a scan. A nurse followed him and after scribbling on my notes, placed them on top of the carrier bag and I was off. At that moment I had absolutely no idea what for or why, all I knew was that I had been bleeding and now I wasn't, but I couldn't wee.

Then there was the pain, even with painkillers it was unbearable and I was feeling very lightheaded. I had no notion of time and felt completely lost.

The CT scanner in the Emergency Department was in use with a patient already waiting so I was taken to the Main X-Ray Department. The waiting room was full, but I was taken straight into a scan room. The radiographer greeted me and explained that they needed to scan my abdomen to check for obstructions. First, I would have to be moved over onto the scan bed. The radiographer was joined by a nurse and I was part rolled, part lifted over. Pain jolted through my back like lightning bolts and they apologised whilst hurriedly lining me up as best they could. My clothing was checked and they discovered my trousers had metal toggles on and so would have to be removed. Those bloody Gwen Stefani's again! Sliding them off they placed a small pillow under my knees to help ease the back pain and the nurse covered me with a blanket because I'd started shaking. Finally, my arms were placed above my head and then they left me alone as the machine whirred into action.

A voice instructed me to breathe in, hold and then breathe normally, as the scan bed moved forward into the tunnel. Lights flashed above me and the instructions sounded again, I felt as though I'd entered a huge tumble dryer. After a couple more times the machine quietened down and I was fed back out of the cylinder.

The nurse joined me once more and explained that she'd need to feed some contrast dye through my veins via the cannula in my arm. This was so that the images would highlight blood vessels and enhance the view of some organs. She warned that as it's fed in, I may experience a sensation like that of having a wee; well as there didn't seem any chance of that I wouldn't worry.

The scanner went through the same procedure again after which the nurse returned with the porter and I was carefully transferred back over to the bed I arrived in. By now the pain was really kicking back in. I had no idea of time let alone what was happening to me. Once again, I watched the fluorescent lights pass above me as the porter navigated the long corridors and took me back to the Emergency Department. He didn't speak. Nobody had said much to me since the paramedics left. Things did not bode well.

CHAPTER 4 THE UNCOMFORTABLE TRUTH

My next destination was a clinical assessment ward which I presumed I'd be in until my results arrived. When a nurse came to check my observations, I asked what was happening. She told me not to worry as a doctor would be along soon. I worried.

I could see only one other patient opposite me in a large square room divided by curtained cubicles. There was a nurse's station near the entrance at which stood three nurses talking quietly but looking over at me. Not quietly enough though as I distinctly overheard one of them say, "She doesn't know yet."

What don't I know? Lying there, I started trying to figure this out. Something was wrong in my kidney area. My Dad had suffered with crippling pain from kidney stones when he was alive, it was a heart attack that killed him at only 41 but before that it was his kidney's that gave him trouble. Did I have a kidney stone? Could a kidney stone cause your kidney to bleed? It must be a whopper!

The indiscreet nurse came over. "You're going to be transferred to Central Hospital soon, a doctor is on his way to explain."

All thoughts of grilling her about my condition disappeared when I heard that I'd be on the move. *What about Jay?*

"My husband won't know where I am. He's got my bag and my phone. He's at work, he's coming here after." I was beginning to panic.

"Don't worry we'll contact him, what's the number?"

Blank. "I don't know, it's on my mobile?"

"Where does he work?" She took my hand now. "We will find him and let him know."

I took a deep breath and managed to give the nurse enough detail to find Jay at work and she went away to call. I saw a doctor arrive in the ward and after a brief word with the nurses he came to speak to me.

There was no introduction or small talk.

"We need to move you as soon as possible; the scan has shown a mass in your left kidney and it is haemorrhaging. An ambulance is on its way to take you to Central where you'll go straight to the urology department. There's nothing more we can do for you here. You'll be under the care of a specialist so don't worry. Any questions?"

Another blank. Strange as it sounds, I still didn't realise the severity of the situation. I'd guessed right with kidney, now though I was more concerned about seeing Jay. I shook my head. I'm not sure I wanted to know more until he was with me.

The doctor left as swiftly as he arrived and I was joined again by the nurse. "We've managed to get in contact with your husband, he'll make his way over to Central and see you there." The news that Jay would meet me at Central lifted my spirits, I can't imagine what he must have been thinking on receiving that call.

Another nurse then appeared at my bedside wheeling a small metal trolley. "The Central Hospital have asked for you to be catheterised."

Pardon me? I had a vague idea of what this involved but a quick glance at the trolley contents didn't warm me to the idea. The curtains were drawn but I can't say my dignity remained intact! As accessories go it was no Louis Vuitton, unattractive, uncomfortable, and unpleasant to be seen with but right now it was a necessary addition.

Soon after, two paramedics came in and together with the nurse began the task of moving me over onto another trolley and I was wheeled out to my second ambulance transfer of the morning.

It was now around 4pm and once again the roads were busy with school runs and home time traffic. The ambulance had to negotiate its way through crowded suburban streets before heading into the city centre. Not long before we set off, I'd been administered more pain control drugs but they seemed to have no effect on the searing jabs that shot through my side and back. These weren't helped by the constant jolting of the ambulance and as hard as I tried, I couldn't stop myself from crying out in pain.

The paramedic who sat with me apologised. "I'm afraid this is about the worst vehicle you could be in, it's one of the old Mercedes vans and the suspension's shot." I think he said shot. Either way he was spot on, it felt as though we were off roading!

"Try this." He handed me a mask for gas and air and as I breathed deeply, I was reminded of being in labour, the last time I'd used any. "Ok that's enough."

The mask was taken away and I asked, "How much further?"

"It's not that far, the traffic's just a little heavy right now, we've got the lights on." This did nothing to reassure me as despite the blue lights it felt as though we were crawling – across cobbled stones.

As soon as there was a clearing the siren went on and the ambulance sped onward again before reaching our destination. This time there was no wait, once I'd been trundled out of the van it was straight through the doors and along to a lift. Two floors up and we entered the urology department where I was taken to the nurse's station to be handed over. Once more I was part lifted and rolled onto another bed where the paramedics left me to the care of the ward staff.

When I say left me, that's how it felt. As soon as I entered the ward I had a bad feeling, almost a sense of being an unwelcome guest. When I say care, I mean that in the loosest sense of the word and it wouldn't be long before this became more evident.

Taken from my medical notes the following transcription explains why I'd had the lengthy wait in the assessment unit at the District. The urologist there was in theatre which eventually prompted the blue light dash to Central.

13/3/13 14.40pm Report from radiologist.

Renal cystic mass with acute bleeding into ureter. It may be amenable to radiological intervention. Suggest urgent urological opinion and if urology team would like interventional radiologist to intervene, they should contact consultant in intervention suite at the District this afternoon.

Bleep/called referral radiology reg via switchboard x 2 = no response.

Called for advice urology reg via mobile, he is in theatre for 3 hours.

Called urology consultant at Central Hospital.

13/03/13 15.40pm

Asked to be seen by consultant renal mass acute bleeding. Transfer to Central ward 11.

***3-way catheter inserted prepared for blue light transfer.**

**This did not actually happen, a 3-way catheter was not inserted at the District so should not have been included in my notes at this stage.*

CHAPTER 5 LIMBO

At the time, apart from the pain which was constant; rising and falling in waves, I was oblivious as to what care I should be receiving. My arrival at Central was at approximately 17.30pm

Following the paramedics' departure, I was left on a urology ward of six beds, each of them occupied by women of varying ages. My bed was nearest the entrance and from where I lay, I could see nurses passing by as well as patients, men and women. I was tired and I hurt like hell. Eventually one of the nurses came into me and explained that she'd have to change my cannula. Apparently, they can't leave one in that has been inserted by another hospital or paramedics.

The first thing she needed to do was get me into a hospital gown. This procedure involved a health care assistant and between them they had to roll me back and forth while I yelped with each jab of pain. The gown was a washed out green and blue number, standard open at the back issue which didn't matter as I had been supine for the best part of the day. When she'd finished, she hooked me up to a drip and gave me pain relief. It didn't work.

It's only in retrospect that I now know; from my medical notes, that I was given paracetomol rather than morphine which is why the pain didn't improve.

Once again, I was left alone and the next person at my bedside was Jay. Seeing him appear was almost better than morphine, for that moment my pain was cancelled out by relief. He didn't quite know what to do as I must have looked a state, gently he put his arms around me and I cried quietly.

Sitting on the edge of the bed Jay whispered, "What's going on, have they told you anything?"

I shook my head, "Have they said anything to you?"

"Nothing." Jay looked concerned. "Have you seen a doctor?"

I told him that apart from the brief encounters I'd had at the District, no doctor had been near me. For that matter, the nurses were scarce since I'd arrived, I felt like an intruder.

"The pain is awful, it hasn't stopped."

I asked Jay if he could ask for more pain relief. As he got up to find a nurse, a health care assistant came to ask if I wanted a hot drink and a sandwich. She'd been doing the evening meal round and noticed I hadn't been included on the list. I gratefully accepted a cup of tea, the first hot drink I'd had since earlier that morning but I couldn't face food.

Jay returned with a nurse who looked around at the foot of my bed then left again. Returning with a trolley she pushed a syringe through my cannula and asked what time I'd been admitted. I wasn't sure, I had no sense of time I hadn't even noticed it had gone dark outside.

This time the pain relief seemed to kick in and I could stop holding myself as tense. Jay produced a rucksack with a few essentials he'd put together with Ruby's help. A flannel, towel, toothbrush and toothpaste. There was a magazine, my phone charger and purse. I gave the purse back, there didn't appear to be anywhere safe to keep it and I wouldn't need money anyway.

Our youngest daughter, Ruby had been working nights on a ward at the General Hospital. She still lived at home with us and so hadn't arrived back until after we'd left that morning. Oblivious to what was happening she'd gone straight to bed. Jay explained how he'd text her that afternoon saying, "I've got to go to Central Hospital later, Mom's been taken ill. Don't worry, speak later."

When she woke up and read the text, Ruby interpreted it as my Mother-in-Law having been taken ill, not me. She messaged him back saying to send her love and asking, "Where's Mom?"

Our eldest, Joey was also working at the General Hospital on a day shift. As she was in A&E I had made sure this wasn't going to be my destination earlier, it would've been awful had I turned up there unannounced and in such a bad way.

Jay and I decided that until we knew more, we wouldn't tell anyone else what was happening. I particularly didn't want to let my Mom know right now, she'd panic and I wouldn't be able to reassure her.

Too soon, it was time for Jay to leave. We both felt an awkward kind of limbo because no one was telling us why I was in. I'd not seen a doctor since arriving at Central and had hoped one would appear while Jay was with me. We were aware there was a mass in my kidney but had no idea what this could be and presumed it was a stone of some kind. My pain wasn't under control either so I felt awful, it was so hard for Jay to leave me that way.

Alone again, I glanced at my phone, the first time since that morning in bed. I'd had texts back from both Sam and Shiraz with understanding comments and the measured number of kisses. I smiled to myself. My social media feed had been unusually silent today, normally filled with fashion related content to mirror the business. I certainly wouldn't be hashtagging my 'Outfit of the Day' right now!

CHAPTER 6 A NEW ACCESSORY

Not long after visiting time the health care assistant returned to give out hot drinks, I couldn't face one. I'm not sure whether it was pain or the painkillers, but I felt quite sick. Shortly after this the lights were dimmed.

I'd been shown how to call for help should I need it, a thick cable ran behind my bed and a call button was attached which hung by my pillow. I'd been looking at this for a while but as I already felt like a nuisance, I was reluctant to use it. Instead I waited for a nurse to pass by, but none appeared. When I could stand the pain no longer, I pushed the button.

The nurse that came apologised for being so long, they'd been changing shift. She looked puzzled checking the notes at the foot of my bed, "I'll be back in a moment, don't worry."

Returning with the drugs trolley she administered morphine and then checked my catheter.

"I'm afraid there's a bit of a problem I'm sorry. I'm going to have to set up an irrigation system."

"A what?!"

It transpired that I was supposed to have had a 3-way catheter so that the blood I was losing would be flushed out. This is what had been in the notes made at the District Hospital that morning, but it hadn't been put in. Not only that, this nurse was about to reveal the reason I'd been pretty much left alone since arriving at Central earlier.

"I really am sorry, it seems you weren't fully admitted on arrival!" She looked genuinely apologetic. "I'm not sure how this happened, did no one explain why you were here, what treatment you'd be having?"

I shook my head, I explained how the paramedics had wheeled me in and I'd not had much contact with nursing staff since. I had wondered why I'd not had dinner – or seen a doctor!

Thank goodness this nurse picked up the mistake when she did as once the irrigation tubes were in place I began to feel the relief almost instantly. The results were evident from the rather attractive bag that fed from my catheter and hung by the side of the bed. It was no Louis Vuitton, but that bag was the most welcome accessory I could wish for, if only it had been fitted earlier in the day. I'd like to think I had a high pain threshold but the screaming agony I'd gone through compared to nothing I'd had in my life before.

My nurse saviour then brought in a fresh hospital gown as the green/blue one I was in now looked a tad unsightly. Gently as possible she rolled me out of one and into the other. Promising that my admission oversight would be investigated. The night nurse left me in my fresh gown, a nice washed-out blue number.

The ward light now went out altogether, only the corridors were illuminated. Sleep was not going to come easily though as the noises around me were constant. Staff talking, patients crying, machines buzzing and bleeping. As tired as I felt, my mind was in overdrive, this time last night I'd gone to bed healthy; or so I'd thought. How, why, what was happening to me? I closed my eyes.

I'm not sure how long I'd slept but it was pain that woke me up. This time not only in my back but also low down near my groin. It was horrendous! The call buzzer lay on top of my bed and I pushed it without hesitation. What seemed like several minutes passed but may have been only a couple, the pain was intense, I was scared. I pushed again, this time calling out, "Help please."

A different nurse walked through, "What's the problem?"

"Pain, here." I pointed. My back hurt so much I couldn't double up or position myself at all in any way to alleviate the burning and throbbing that pulsed through me.

Coming to the side of my bed the nurse checked the catheter and drain bags. Both were full; not only that, the drain tube was blocked with blood clots. She removed the bags, replacing them with fresh and then began manipulating the tubes which eventually freed the clots and I felt a sudden rushing sensation and the pain subsided. I cried with relief.

"It's ok," she said, "they can get blocked sometimes, all you have to do is wiggle them about so don't worry. I'll top up your morphine."

At the time I was so grateful for her intervention it didn't occur to me that tube wiggling may be a nursing job. I didn't question why the catheter bags had been left to fill to capacity because I was just thankful the pain had decreased. Sleep once again found me. Morning woke me too soon.

CHAPTER 7 DAY 2 THE C WORD

The lights went on at 6.30am and soon afterwards the hot drinks trolley made its round. Almost simultaneously a health care assistant trundled the large breakfast trolley in. I still felt sick but not having eaten for so long I was extremely hungry. No one had advised against eating, so I ordered some rice crispies and a cup of coffee.

It was while I was eating cereal that a young registrar appeared. He was doing ward rounds and stopped at the foot of my bed to read my notes.

"Good morning." He smiled, moving forward to stand at the side of the bed. Without introducing himself he continued.

"We need to arrange surgery to remove the cancer."

Freeze frame!

I'm propped up in a hospital bed wearing a pale blue gown holding a bowl of rice crispies and a spoon. I haven't washed for a day and my hair needs bleaching. I'm alone; completely alone apart from a trainee consultant whose name I don't know and he's just casually let slip that I have CANCER!?

I must have looked completely vacant. This was not how news of this kind was supposed to be delivered. I've watched Casualty, you could at least sit down and get a nurse to hold my hand. Shouldn't you have called my husband? Have you got the right patient only there have been a few mistakes already? Questions ran through my brain, but words never made it out of my mouth. I think I asked if it was in my kidney, silly question but this was a silly situation. This was downright feckin' ridiculous!

The registrar looked uncomfortable. "You didn't know?"

I shook my head. Should I be crying? I didn't feel like crying I felt angry.

He apologised. "I'm so sorry, I was told to come and explain your next treatment." He looked embarrassed. "You will be sent to have an embolisation, an interventional radiologist will perform the procedure which will stop the tumour bleeding."

Behind him, the woman in the bed opposite me was vomiting into a cardboard bowl, no one was with her. I wanted to point it out, I wanted to stop listening. I wanted to go home.

"Well, I'll erm get a nurse to come in and go through what the embolisation will involve." He was squirming now.

All I could think was, *she must've filled the bowl by now. Someone must have heard her?* My mind had switched off completely from my own predicament and was focussed on the woman throwing up.

The registrar pulled the curtain behind him and I sat, rice crispies in my lap and spoon still in hand. No tears.

Now I may be a little naïve but I'm sure this isn't how bad news is delivered on Holby City. Aren't relatives supposed to be present? Don't they take them into a side room and explain the seriousness of the condition? This is not how the C word should be presented. I mean, no introduction, no fanfare just that word aimed at me.

A sister drew back the curtain, her face like thunder. She took the cereal bowl from me and asked what I'd just been told.

"I've got cancer, in my kidney."

"I'll be right back." The sister turned on her heel and dashed out. I could hear raised voices but couldn't make out the conversation, vomiting woman had started again.

In came the sister and taking both my hands she spoke slowly looking me in the eyes. "I'm so sorry, he had no right to break that news to you alone, you must be feeling very distressed?"

"I don't know what to feel, it's happening too fast, I didn't expect this. I need to tell my husband."

She was a kind nurse and appeared upset by my treatment but didn't have the time to stay longer. The woman opposite couldn't stop heaving and now the woman next to her was pushing the buzzer repeatedly. In the corridor a man was walking around naked and there was a phone somewhere ringing off the hook.

"I really am sorry." Now she was glancing over at vomiting lady.

"It's fine, I'll be ok."

I wasn't ok.

Lunchtime came and went. I couldn't face food. I tried to imagine what I'd be doing if I weren't in a hospital bed but weirdly, I couldn't think. Even though it had only been a little over 24 hours I felt as though this was routine. My life had altered immeasurably since yesterday, it was as though I'd been placed in a parallel universe and there was no way back.

I must have dozed off and I awoke to voices next to me. Another doctor in a dark pinstriped suit was speaking to a nurse at the foot of my bed.

Maybe it was the morphine which was now being topped up regularly or it could've been that I'd just woken up, I felt as though I was still dreaming.

The doctor held out his hand. "I'm Mr Collins, consultant surgeon. You won't be my patient; you're going to be in the care of Mr Richards however he's not on shift today."

I shook his hand, real enough.

"Now I gather you've been notified of the tumour in your left kidney?"

You could say that. I nodded.

"Mr Richards will be removing that just as soon as we've stopped the bleeding. Has the embolisation procedure been explained to you?"

I shook my head. Hospital was rendering me mute.

"An interventional radiologist will perform the embolisation which will cut off the flow of blood to the tumour. We estimate the size to be about 7cm and it's currently haemorrhaging so we need to stop this as soon as possible. We've booked you in for this to be done tomorrow."

I was awake now.

"Any questions?"

I shook myself from the dream like state I'd been in.

"How do you know it's cancer, I've not had a biopsy?"

"We can tell from your scan."

He kept my gaze for a moment and then turning to the nurse, "Chase up radiology and make sure she's on the list tomorrow."

Then they were gone.

Nothing was as it was supposed to be. Nothing would be the same again.

CHAPTER 8 FAMILY GATHERING

At visiting time Jay arrived with both our girls; the first time I'd seen them since the morning before. They gathered around my bed and we hugged, the girls were visibly upset. Despite both being nurses in a familiar environment, they were not prepared for seeing me in a hospital bed hooked up to so much equipment.

Questions came quickly; how did I feel, who had I seen, what did they say? I looked at Jay frowning, this was too hard. Without words he understood.

"Girls, go and see if there's a drinks machine," handing them cash he walked them out to the corridor and returned, drawing the curtain around us. "Tell me."

Only eleven days previously we had been in London celebrating our twenty-fifth wedding anniversary. That weekend Jay and I had walked for miles across the capital sightseeing. It had been the most amazing weekend; we'd taken lots of photos and I'd felt fantastic. In twenty-five years of marriage we'd gained two beautiful daughters, a lovely home, an unbreakable bond and a joint telepathy.

Now as I held his gaze it was this sixth sense that travelled from me to him. That awful news, the knowledge of a life-threatening disease that weighed so heavy was lifted as Jay nodded his head.

Cancer.

I don't even remember the word being said.

The girls returned and chatted about work, commenting on what they noticed around the ward. They weren't impressed. It amused me to see them checking my notes and questioning my treatment. Ruby called a nurse in to change my catheter bag, which was fit to burst once more, I could've done with her the night before.

Jay said that he and the girls had visited my Mom before coming to me. All they told her was that I was in hospital having tests on my kidney. To be fair that was the truth, but it was enough for my Mom to be worried sick.

I remembered that my father suffered with kidney stones when I was a child and the pain he went through. My Dad didn't live for many years after, it wasn't his kidneys though but his heart that took him away. He came home one evening feeling unwell and within minutes had a heart attack. The doctor's said he didn't stand a chance it was a huge blood clot, he died at home that night and I heard it all through my bedroom wall. An eerie rasping sound that I now know to have been my Dad fighting to breathe. Voices of neighbours, one attempting CPR. The sound of my Mom shouting at the paramedics in the street. "You're too bloody late!" The click of my bedroom door being pulled to; I watched the handle moving as someone on the other side held it closed. Crying, lots of crying and whispering, people pacing back and forth. Apparently, police came, its procedure, they checked Mom and Dad's bedroom and asked questions. "Why was there a bowl and towel by the bed? Why had my Dad drunk indigestion medicine? Who was present?" Loads of questions my Mom was in no state to answer.

Dad had come home feeling sick, he had chest pains but put it down to heart burn and swigged some milk of magnesia from the bottle. Mom found him lying on the floor in the living room and managed to get him upstairs into bed. She'd placed a towel across him and brought in a bowl in case he vomited. He lost consciousness soon after and so she'd dialled 999 and shouted the neighbours for help.

In the meantime, I'd woken confused about the noises I could hear. I needed a wee but was too worried to go onto the landing, so I lay awake, I heard it all. For hours I lay there; desperate for a wee, silently crying for my Dad, knowing why but somehow not believing. Maybe I'd got it wrong? If I left the bed though I'd know for sure and so there I stayed, paralysed with fear and guilt. Guilt, because I hadn't moved, what if he needed me? I was afraid.

It was March 21st when he came home unwell and the early hours of the 22nd that he died. For me it was the longest night of my life and whilst the memories of my Dad's last breaths will remain with me always so will the memory of needing to wee. When my bedroom door was finally pushed open I felt a wave of relief and fear. I know my Mom was knelt beside me crying, telling me my Dad had died. I recall my Auntie behind her. I also remember wanting them to move so I could run to the loo. That base function, the need to pee ruining a most delicate and tragic moment. Is there ever a good moment to tell a child their father is dead?

Now, as I looked at my daughters, their faces taught with concern, cheeks tear stained and brows furrowed I thought, *is there ever a good time to tell your children you have cancer?*

The C word wasn't mentioned and when the time came for them to leave there was only one issue to sort. Who to tell, or rather who not to tell in the circle of family and friends?

I still wanted to keep my illness quiet until I'd come to terms with it myself, Jay agreed. We decided close family only for the time being, anyone else on a need-to-know basis.

I didn't want them to leave, after that first night I was afraid of being alone. Trying my hardest not to cry I hugged the girls close, they walked on ahead leaving J holding my hands.

"I'll be ok." I did my best to reassure Jay. I watched as he disappeared out into the corridor and waited until I heard the swoosh of the swing doors close behind him. Now my tears fell, I cried as though I would never stop.

CHAPTER 9 NIGHTMARE

Dinner came and went. I ate mostly a vegetarian diet – I could be tempted by a bacon sandwich now and again, but meat was off the menu most of the time. The choice of meat free meals wasn't overly exciting, cheese pie or salad. I opted for the cheese pie which had the familiar taste of Smash, those potato granules in a packet popular in the seventies. Thankfully, vomiting lady had left us, mealtimes weren't pleasant when accompanied by the sound of heaving. I was now opposite a young lady who was very tearful and refused her dinner requesting the curtains be drawn around her. Next to me was an elderly lady called Muriel, she was a feisty old dear and very vocal about the quality of the food we'd been served up.

"It's like slop," she complained having opted for shepherd's pie which swam across her plate as she attempted to spoon it up.

"My dog would turn his nose up at this." Muriel's neighbour Clara agreed.

"It's either one way or the other, yesterday we had chicken and it brought my teeth out!" The image conjured up by Clara wasn't helping my own appetite.

The bed opposite Muriel was empty, the lady who had occupied it earlier had been taken down for surgery. Next to her was another younger lady who couldn't speak any English and refused the hospital food. Her family were still present in the corridor, there had been some confusion about the numbers allowed in at visiting time, eleven had turned up. During mealtime one family member was allowed in to bring her food from the canteen which she ate with the curtains drawn. This did not draw approval from Muriel and Clara and they whispered and tutted between themselves.

After dinner, the time dragged. I now had my phone which I'd managed to charge using the plug socket behind my bed. Scrolling through my social media accounts didn't lighten my mood, life was going on as normal. No-one knew where I was, that's how I wanted it. There was no way I'd be posting Facebook updates 'Checking in to Central Hospital' or 'Had the worst news'. Those status' begging myriads of questions from curious acquaintances was not my style; and my style right now was totally not worthy of a selfie. I hadn't been out of the hospital bed since arrival - catheterisation was a weird experience to say the least and I hadn't seen a mirror.

I'd had a few texts but nothing that needed answering right away. Sam had returned with get well wishes and the obligatory three kisses. Shiraz had replied similarly and also attached three kisses, now I'd have to match him, I didn't want to upset one of the best models I had. There was also a text from one of my Clothes Show customers, I was working on a rather unfortunately named Sidebutt Catsuit for her, a Gwen Stefani number – that woman was vexing me. For the past couple of years, I'd had my own stand at the Clothes Show Live Exhibition in the NEC Birmingham, it was one of my biggest earning opportunities. December 2012 had been an excellent show; I'd sold loads over the week and taken plenty of private commission orders. Little did I know it would be the last time my business exhibited there, especially as I was doing so well. The customer, Caroline wanted to know when I'd be sending the catsuit as I'd already informed her it was almost finished. What could I say? What could I do? I suppose I could ask Sam, but I didn't want to worry her. There was a lot of pressure attached to private commission orders; customers who paid a lot expected perfection. It was down to me to deliver that, but I could hardly oblige from a hospital bed, the only thing I could do was to put the phone away. I didn't even bother looking at the emails. Work was something I had no control over, I had to push it to the back of my mind, for now.

I returned the phone to my bag which sat in the top of the cabinet next to my bed. The girls had brought magazines and I had a book to read but I couldn't focus my mind on anything, so I closed my eyes.

I must have slept because when I woke there was a lot of noise in the corridor outside. The lights had dimmed so it was past 9pm. I couldn't figure out what was happening in the ward, but I did know that the pain in my side had increased. As my eyes adjusted to the gloom, I saw that all but Muriel and Clara were sleeping, those two had struck up quite a friendship and were currently deliberating about the commotion outside.

I pushed my buzzer; the pain was unbearable.

"You'll be lucky," Muriel advised in a hoarse whisper. "That lot are up to something."

"I just need more pain relief." My voice also came out as a whisper, my throat was incredibly dry.

"Clara needed the toilet half an hour ago and they've still not taken her."

Clara cut in. "I need twos."

Too much information.

"At last, we've been buzzing you for ages." Muriel addressed the two nurses that made their way into the ward closely followed by two HCA's. "We've got the whole gang now; Clara needs the toilet." One of the HCA's drew the curtains around Clara while the others continued their conversation which sounded like a plan to move us around.

"Can I please have some more pain relief." I found myself putting my hand up like a school child.

One of the nurses came to the foot of my bed. "I'll be with you in just a moment." She wasn't even looking at me. The curtain drew back around Clara and once the HCA had deposited her erm, deposit, the four members of staff gathered around Muriel's bed.

"Ok this one first." They each took a corner and began moving the bed away from the wall. "Ok Muriel we're just going a couple of bays along hold on tight."

Poor Muriel looked terrified. "What do you mean, why have I got to move, what about Clara?"

"It's only down the corridor, we have to manage our admissions I'm afraid." The nursing staff moved swiftly, one taking the bedside cabinet and another unhooking Muriels' drip and arranging tubes while the other two guided the bed out of our bay.

"It's the middle of the night." Muriel's voice trailed off down the ward while Clara began getting upset.

"I didn't get to say goodbye." I couldn't see her properly in the gloom of the night lights but I'm sure she was crying.

It's an unsettling feeling when you're bed bound and can neither look after yourself nor offer someone else help when they need it. I wanted to give Clara a cuddle, I needed a cuddle and more urgently I wanted some pain relief.

Over the course of the next half hour we were all moved to other parts of the ward, I'm still not sure why. I was wheeled further down the corridor and put next to a window. A nurse topped up my pain relief, but I was still uncomfortable with a fierce burning sensation in my groin. It was then I remembered the tubes, I reached down and began twisting and squeezing them, but nothing alleviated the pain. The bags did seem incredibly full again so once more I pushed the buzzer and a nurse came to sort out changing them. While she was gone, I reached down to get my phone but there was no cabinet. When the nurse returned, I explained my bed had moved but my belongings hadn't, she wasn't pleased and stomped off to find it. An hour must have passed before she returned wheeling the bedside cabinet; she didn't even wait while I checked it was mine. I thought it probably too much to ask her for a replacement jug of water. I was learning that the nursing staff were completely unpredictable; some couldn't do enough for you, others did as little as possible. Thankfully, my bag was in the cupboard and retrieving my phone I scrolled through recent photos. I didn't recognise myself even though they were taken a matter of weeks before. From my hospital bed the images lighting up my phone showed me as a happy, confident businesswoman. If I turned to the window beside my bed the reflection there was of a tired, frightened hospital patient. I put back the phone and as I laid my head down the tears began to come. The surge of emotion that filled me was pure self-pity and I sobbed so hard I had to bury my face in the sheets for fear of waking others. I have never felt so alone in my life.

CHAPTER 10 DAY 3 FALSE START

Staff had been scarce throughout the night probably due to the musical beds and I'd become expert at manipulating the tubes attached to my catheter, freeing the blood clots. During the morning rounds it came as no surprise when a nurse showed concern at how low my blood pressure had fallen, half of it appeared to be in the drainage bag beside me. She hurried off and returned with the sister in charge.

"You will be taken for embolisation later this morning, the bleeding needs to be stopped." The sister was busy writing on my charts while she delivered this news. "I'm afraid you'll need to be nil by mouth until after the procedure."

I still felt quite sick and so going without breakfast didn't upset me, I wasn't sure about what my 'procedure' entailed though. "What will they do to me, will I be awake?" Although the embolisation procedure had been explained I hadn't taken everything in, now it was imminent I needed reassurance.

"You will be awake but won't feel anything, the interventional radiographer will feed a small wire up through your catheter with some tiny beads which will hopefully stop the flow of blood to the tumour. He'll explain fully when you get to the intervention suite. Don't worry." Those last two words were murmured as the sister swept back out onto the ward leaving me with the nurse who gave me a pained expression that read, *I'm really sorry but I have to follow her.* As she too backed out, I was alone again.

I could hear the breakfast trolley clattering along and the other patients in my bay were beginning to sit themselves up. I couldn't imagine what I might look like to them, complete strangers. I certainly didn't look like a fashion designer. The thing that was really bothering me was that I'd still not had a wash since arriving in hospital. I hadn't thought much about it at first, the shock had overwhelmed me and pain cancelled out everything else. Today though I'd had time to begin trying to make sense of it all and come to terms with my situation.

There wasn't a mirror anywhere near, but I imagined my appearance was quite bizarre. Back in December I'd had my hair cut into a Mohican and dyed pink, prior to that I'd had multicoloured dreadlocks for seven years. When I'd booked the last Clothes Show Exhibition, I wanted a whole new look. I took out my dreadlocks and visited my friend, Nicky who is a fantastic hairdresser and I asked her to shave the sides of my hair; I was her first Mohican. It looked great though and certainly made an impact at the time. Winter wasn't a good month for a Mohican haircut though, if I put a hat on in cold weather it never quite recovered so I decided to grow it out.

Now, sitting in my hospital bed with an untidy Mohican and dark roots with pink tips I must have looked terrible. God knows what state the rest of me was in, it was a good job the sheets came up high. The next time a nurse came by I asked about having a wash, she pointed me in the direction of the bathroom and said go ahead. This took me by surprise as I'd not left the bed at all since arriving. Despite disliking being immobile I was also scared about getting on my feet. More than that I didn't fancy asking the staff for help, the feeling of being a burden still lingered. There was nothing else for it, I had to have a wash.

Slowly I slid each leg to the edge of the bed and then hung them down, pushing myself up onto my left arm. The pain was more controlled, but that movement sent pangs tearing up my left side taking my breath. Resting my head on the pillow I took a few deep breaths and then pushed up again to a sitting position. The small cabinet beside the bed held my belongings from which I took my wash bag. Now for the real test, I gently lowered my feet to the floor and raised myself to standing.

"You shouldn't be doing that Bab." The lady in the bed opposite spoke for the first time. We'd made eye contact and smiled but until now there had been no conversation on the ward. Odd really? My bathroom adventure had gained her interest though. "You wanna ring yer buzzer and get a nurse to help you." She heaved herself higher on her pillows to get a better look at my predicament.

"I've asked thanks, but I was told to go myself." By now I'd wobbled back onto the bed.

"How're you gonna push your gear with you?" She pointed at my drip and drain bags.

"Well, I'm about to figure that out, I don't think I'll get any help to be honest." I managed to raise myself back up, hooking the wash bag over my arm I took hold of the drip stand with my left hand and drain with the right.

"You'll end up in a heap if you're not careful." She was shaking her head so vigorously she nearly lost her teeth.

"Shame innit?" They were all coming to life now. The lady in the bed next to my advisor appeared from under the covers, it was Muriel. "You'd think they come and give 'er a hand?"

Great now I had an audience for my first attempt at walking for three days. The stands that held the drip and drain were on wheels, they resembled tall coat hooks but held bags of saline and in my case blood stained wee. I figured that if I pushed them along, one at a time they'd serve as crutches, kind of land skiing with unpleasant poles.

I glanced to my left, the woman in the bed next to me was asleep, just the beds opposite to cheerlead me on. It dawned on me then I had no footwear, I'd have to go barefoot. Although it was a hospital and should therefore be a clean environment, I didn't like the idea of walking around with nothing on my feet.

As I moved gradually along, I received words of encouragement from Muriel and her new pal who appeared to be enjoying the activity. Reaching the curtains that divided the ward from the corridor I met with a nurse, I smiled a meek, *help me* smile. She walked past. Ahead of me I could see a toilet sign and struggled towards it, I was beginning to get into a rhythm with my skis. Nearly there I met another nurse.

"Where are you going?" I felt like a naughty child.

"I need a wash, I did ask if I could." Maybe she'd give me a hand.

"Oh right, well the bathrooms in the other direction." The nurse pointed me back along the corridor. "This is only a toilet, there is a hand basin though." I think she saw the look of dismay cross my face at the thought of walking further.

"Ok thanks." I waited for her to walk on and pushed open the toilet door. There was a small hand basin, that'd do for now. I never knew washing my face could feel so good. I had to avoid the cannula in the back of my hand so getting to my armpits wasn't easy. I gave up in the end and my hair would have to wait.

It was also the first time I'd seen myself in a mirror since being admitted. God, I looked rough. I took out my toothbrush, at least I could clean my teeth, that was a relief. The rest of me would have to remain under the sheets. No one would be checking the length of my leg hair!

By the time I'd made my way back to the bed my neighbours were chattering away, even the lady next to me had joined in. The general topic was how poor the care had been. Muriel's new friend was called Betty and both had kidney infections. The other lady had kidney stones and the patients in the other two beds remained sleeping.

I didn't feel very sociable and so reached for my phone. I really needed to make a decision concerning work and what to do about my current order book. Amongst the messages was a text from my cousin Sue, she only lived a stone's throw from the hospital, but I still didn't want to let more people know, even family. There was a missed call and voicemail from my friend Fi asking if I wanted a trip into Birmingham for fabrics next week. We always left each other silly messages, as I listened, she sang a made-up song about walking her dog Hector. I'd only seen her a few days ago and yet hearing her voice it could have been weeks. Being in hospital was like entering a time warp, I felt as though I was trapped in a bubble looking out at a world I couldn't reach.

I scrolled down the lengthy list of emails deleting as I went, most were trash. I stopped at another message from Caroline wanting to know the progress of her side-butt catsuit. As designs go it was a head turner. A black, velvet catsuit with mesh panels that ran from the ankles up the sides of both legs then low across the back. The mesh continued over the shoulders and down to the cleavage, both sleeves were all mesh. Underwear was not an option... I'd taken the commission on when she told me she wanted to wear it to her graduation party, in Wolverhampton. Now that's brave! Unfortunately, the event was that coming weekend and there was no way she'd be making her entrance in my design mores' the pity. Gwen Stefani was really making her mark in my life right now.

I felt incredibly guilty typing out my reply to Caroline, I would be letting her down big time and that was something I didn't do. Working for myself was extremely rewarding but the hardest job was maintaining a good reputation. Regardless of the reason, this would be damaging and I felt bad. As I pressed send, I felt a huge pang of guilt and a feeling of helplessness, I was losing control.

Continuing down the emails I'd had two sales via my website and another on eBay, great normally. This wasn't good though, they'd need packaging and sending, I had a routine. I turned my phone off again, I couldn't deal with this now, business wasn't possible from a hospital bed, I was feeling anxious.

The rattle of plates on a trolley signalled the start of the lunch round. I'd had no news about my embolisation, the morning booking had now slipped seamlessly into afternoon and I was beginning to feel quite hungry. Forbidden from eating, I turned myself away. Closing my eyes, I tried to relax, I must have drifted to sleep. I'm not sure how long I'd slept but the sky outside was already growing dark when a voice brought me back to reality,

"Mrs Murphy, we've received notification that your embolisation will proceed at 8.30am tomorrow morning." The doctor who addressed me was now looking at the Nil by Mouth label that hung behind my bed and waved a clipboard in that direction. "What's all this about?"

"I was told this morning that I'd be taken for embolisation and so I've not had anything to eat," I explained. The doctor asked who it was gave me this information. "The sister on duty this morning." *Oh no... not another mistake...?*

"Well, I've no idea where she heard that, but your procedure has only just been booked in. Are you telling me that you've had nothing at all to eat today?" I nodded my head and he paced off towards the nurse station. Raised voices could be heard before he strode back in. "I've arranged for some sandwiches to be made up for you and a hot drink, I can only apologise."

"It's ok." Well what else could I say? I was worried about complaining while I remained under the care of the ward staff and even their good books that didn't count for much.

From my bed I observed the hospital, a clinical soundscape of bleeps and buzzers, clatter and chatter. It was hard to keep track of time, night-times merely dimmed, the only blackout in hospital is of the medical kind. Harsh lighting left nowhere to hide and silence never visited these wards. I reached for the magazines the girls had brought me, within one of the cellophane wrappers was a free notepad and pen. Opening a blank page, I wrote, Wednesday 13th March 2013, woke feeling unwell. By the time I'd brought my hospital journal up to date the evening drinks trolley was beginning its rounds; soon the lights would go down, night would clatter into day and I would turn over a page, pen poised to keep track of events to save losing my grip on reality.

CHAPTER 11 THE F WARD

My third night came and went. I'd become adept at manipulating the tubes that fed into my catheter bag. Using the buzzer seemed only to annoy night staff and the consensus was to buzz as little as possible. Muriel however took exception to this and buzzed even when another patient needed attention. It was the sound of the buzzer that woke me early next morning. One continuous buzz coming from along the corridor. Opening my eyes, I saw the other occupants of my bay all waking and wondering what was happening, and then it started. The loudest, angriest, most foul-mouthed tirade of abuse I'd ever heard coming from the bay next door.

"You lazy fucking bitches. How long are you going to leave me like this? You idle bastards. I've been buzzing for nearly a fucking hour. How much longer do you want me to sit in shit?!"

On and on like this, the man shouting hardly drew breath until he ended with a finale that included the C word – not Cancer. The ward went quiet momentarily until Betty started clapping. "I really enjoyed that," she laughed, "it's just what they need, a good kick up the arse."

Despite the poor man's obvious predicament, we all enjoyed his entertaining wake up call. I'd almost forgotten my looming embolisation. The sound of the breakfast trolley reminded me I'd be nil by mouth again, so I was surprised when asked what cereal I'd like.

"I've got an embolisation this morning should I be eating?" I questioned the HCA serving breakfast. She looked at her list and confirmed I was on it but went away to find out. The sister that returned with her was becoming known to us as a woman who lacked both bedside manner and patience.

"I'd have thought you'd be wanting breakfast after yesterday?" The doctor's complaint on my behalf had not gone unnoticed. She flipped my charts over swiftly then hooked them back on the end of the bed. "There's nothing here says your nil by mouth, so you'd best eat as you'll not be wanting anything after your op."

I thanked her for the confidence boost and accepted a bowl of rice crispies from the hovering HCA whose round I was holding up. Even Muriel's bowel movements couldn't put me off eating this morning, breakfast was the only meal that resembled anything like the food I'd eat at home.

Not long after breakfast a porter arrived to take me down for the embolisation. My bed was wheeled into the lift and taken to the radiology department; first stop a small windowless room where I met the interventional radiologist who was to perform the procedure. He shook my hand and introduced himself. A gently spoken man, he went on to explain properly what was going to happen. The tumour in my kidney was still bleeding and so they needed a way to stop it before I went for surgery. The radiologist explained how he would feed a thin plastic tube (catheter) into my groin which would then need to find the artery that was supplying blood to the tumour. He would be guided by digital images showing the progress of the tube which would wind its way up the blood vessel and inject some tiny beads that would block the blood supply to the tumour. He warned that this was a process that could fail but if it succeeded then the tumour would also shrink. I had to sign paperwork to confirm I understood, not only the procedure but also the risks. I don't remember exactly what they were, but I recall feeling afraid. Jay would have no idea what was happening as he couldn't be there until visiting time, I felt so helpless.

After doing his best to reassure me the radiologist left me in the care of a couple of nurses who changed me into another gown opening at the front. One nurse sighed heavily when she saw I had pants on.

"Why do they always send them in underwear?" She began taking them off while the other stood shaking her head as if it were the most ridiculous thing she'd seen.

"I know, that ward do as little as possible." Their conversation carried on above my head while I lost more than a little dignity. Going through my notes one asked when I'd last eaten so I told them only about an hour ago, my cereal.

"What?" The nurse looked furious. "Why did you take breakfast, you're nil by mouth?" She was blaming me!

"I asked on the ward, but they told me I could." My tears were coming.

"What else did you have?" She stood pen poised.

"A coffee, I did ask if I could."

Giving a huge sigh the nurse swooshed out of the swing doors while the other tossed my pants into what appeared to be a waste bin, charming. The radiologist couldn't have been too concerned about my rice crispies as, soon after I was wheeled out into the corridor and over to a room marked theatre. Now shit was getting real.

Inside it was very dark and warm, my bed was positioned underneath a large scanner alongside what looked like TV screens.

"You'll be awake throughout the procedure although we'll numb the area around your groin." The radiologist smiled reassuringly. "If you want to, you can watch what we're doing on the screen here." I turned my head and could already see myself lying on the bed. "Right, one last thing." He walked across to a CD player and put on some music. To my amazement the track that began playing was an Irish fiddle tune, Return to Erin, one that I played myself and brought back fond memories. "Ready?"

"Ready."

The embolisation itself was relatively painless. I felt the catheter being fed into the artery in my thigh and watched its progress on the screen. I can't say that I felt anything actually happening inside me, but it was both fascinating and terrifying to actually see the tumour. I'm not sure how long it took either, I felt so tired afterwards that I struggled to stay awake. The radiologist was so concerned about me that he wheeled my bed all the way back to the ward, I was extremely touched by this. Up until then my hospital experience hadn't been at all what I was expecting. I don't suppose medical school can teach empathy. However, this man understood how I must have been feeling and his actions meant a great deal to me. I found out from a member of his team that the radiologist didn't usually work Saturdays, but my case had been marked urgent, so he'd been called in specially. I will always be grateful for his expertise and care.

I spent most of the rest of the day sleeping. When I woke Jay was sitting next to me, I hadn't heard him arrive and not much visiting time was left. I relayed what I could of the embolisation but mostly we talked about home and the girls. When it was time for him to leave, I got terribly upset, it's odd how hospital life was somehow already becoming the norm. Reality seemed to be drifting away from me. For Jay, the trip over to see me was awful. The hospital was in East Birmingham and the round trip from his work and then back home took nearly two hours in busy traffic. Saying goodbye became more difficult each time.

Before settling down for the night I returned to my notebook, carefully recording the day's proceedings. As I wrote I smiled, overhearing Betty and Muriel commenting on my scribbling.

"She's up to something." Muriel was telling her friend. "Been getting that little book out and taking notes."

"She wants to be careful that lot don't get wind of it." Betty nodded towards the nurse's station, "She'll be out on her ear."

It wouldn't be long before Betty's prophesy would be coming true.

CHAPTER 12 DAY 5 HOLDING HANDS

It was 2am, I was wide awake.

The date was March 17th, St Patrick's Day. I smiled, normally this would be a day of celebration, dancing and singing. For years we'd held our own St Patrick's Day parties, the house would be full of friends and neighbours. Along with many of our friends we played and sang, I played fiddle and Jay guitar, mainly folk and Irish music. The St Pat's parties would have a regular theme; music and alcohol, both were plentiful. As we often played in sessions at a local club, we'd acquired pub banners, flags, etc so our home would be decked out in the green, white and gold. Thinking about these parties I realised that we would have held one on the previous night, in fact it would be still have been going, they generally went on 'till at least 5am. Jay had mentioned that he'd told a few people I was unwell but hadn't said what with or where I was. No wonder I'd had so many texts, people were missing the party.

Each year we went to the St Patrick's Day Parade in Birmingham as a family, this is always held on the Sunday before the 17th. After Dublin and New York, Birmingham hosts the third biggest parade in the world and it's one of our favourite events in the calendar. This year though the 17th fell on a Sunday, *today*. As the realisation dawned on me there was a lump in my throat, I would miss the parade.

I took my phone from my bag; I hadn't even looked at it since the day before as I'd been rather preoccupied. Switching on, the messages began lighting up. Questions: *Where are you? Hope you're ok? Been trying to call. What are you up to?* Then of course*, Will you be at the parade tomorrow?* Guilt overcame me; I'd been ignoring my friends those last few days. It was easier not to answer than to lie to them. What could I say though? The last thing I wanted was a stream of visitors, there were so many questions I couldn't and didn't know the answer to myself. No, I was doing the right thing. Until I was able to cope with the situation no one else could know. I switched off.

It was difficult to settle back down. A young girl had been moved into the bed opposite me and was crying on and off while the lady next to Muriel was vomiting. Muriel however slept like a baby. Things somehow always seem worse in the middle of the night, but I was about to hit a new low. A nurse came to attend to vomiting lady then across to see to the tearful girl. Glancing over at my bed she looked puzzled and came over to check the drain bag beside me. I was bleeding.

The nurse did her best to reassure me. "Sometimes it's not a new bleed, we'll keep an eye on things but hopefully it'll be clear again in a few hours." Audrey, the nurse looked to be a similar age to me and as she spoke, stroked my hand. "You've really been through the mill, haven't you?" Reading my notes, she frowned. "Has anyone spoken to you about your cancer or mentioned surgery?"

I shook my head. "Apparently the surgeon's on holiday, I haven't got a date, don't know much really."

"We need to do something about this." Audrey replaced my notes and tucked me in. "I'm working till lunchtime tomorrow, I'll make sure you get your answers. Try and sleep, I'm here if you need me." Audrey was an angel. She made me feel safe for the first time since arriving and now I had something to hope for... answers.

The dark night was replaced by a grey morning. My view took in an industrial scene, chimneys and warehouse roofs. There was a flutter of snow, I hoped it would clear before the parade later; even though I wouldn't be there I wanted it to be a great day. The texts began arriving early.

'Happy St Patricks Day! Have one (or several) for me.'

'Let me know when you're in Digbeth, we'll try and meet for a pint.'

'How's your head, ready for round two?'

My friend Fi text. 'I won't make it today so thought I'd better text you now as you'll be out of it by lunchtime!' With the amounts of morphine currently coursing through my veins, she wasn't far wrong.

The lights were raised and the clatter of breakfast soon woke the other patients. I looked down at the drain bag, was it looking paler, had the bleeding stopped? As if reading my thoughts Audrey appeared again.

"That's looking healthier," she smiled. "I reckon it was merely a blip, happens sometimes." Coming closer, Audrey leant into me. "Is your husband available at all today?" I looked at her puzzled and she explained. "I can give him a call and allow him in early, I'll sort out a wheelchair and he can take you off the ward for a little while, give you time to talk." I nodded overwhelmed, we hadn't had a chance to speak properly about the blow we'd been dealt, it's not easy when you're overheard and scrutinised by all around you.

"Thank you. Do you want my husband's number?" I took out my phone and Audrey jotted it down.

"It's best I call him, I'll need to let him in and sort the chair, leave it with me." She winked and turned her attention to the multitude of buzzers sounding along the ward.

As the morning crept on the clouds began to lift, the sun was doing its best to make an appearance at the parade. A young Irish registrar came to see me on the ward rounds, he was wearing a Kilkenny Gaelic football top so was probably planning on celebrating later.

"Audrey says you have some questions that need answering?" I nodded as he continued. "Have a think about what you need to know and write it down, I'll come back tomorrow and do my best to give you answers." I thanked him; he was going to have a pretty long list so had better not have too many for the road!

Soon after, Jay arrived which set tongues wagging in the bay, what had I done to deserve company out of visiting hours? Audrey had to go and find a wheelchair; all the ones from our ward had 'gone missing' which was apparently common. She'd phoned another couple of wards, but they weren't helpful, wheelchairs were a rare commodity. Eventually she appeared with one and helped me climb in, covering me with a blanket. I only had the trainers that I'd arrived in, so they were put on too along with my fleece jacket. I didn't know what to do with my feet, then Audrey slid out to foot plates from under the chair, we couldn't stop laughing. It's hard not to fall into a Lou and Andy routine when you're covered with a blanket and wheeled off in a chair.

"If anyone asks, you know nothing about the chair," she warned. "Now take your time, have a wander down to the café, it might even be ok outside if you want a breath of fresh air."

Opening the main doors, she waved us off, freedom.

Jay pushed me down the to the café where we sat and had a hot chocolate, a far cry from the pints of Guinness we should have in front of us. It wasn't a comfortable environment, rather than hospital staff or visitors it seemed to be a local meeting place as a large number of men had virtually taken over one corner of the café and were having a loud discussion. We decided to brave the elements, the sun hadn't made it through and the wind was whipping up, but it was good to be out of the hospital. Wheelchairs were a first for us both, Jay manoeuvring and me as a passenger. There were few pathways around and those we found were extremely uneven, not ideal when you're in pain. The hospital grounds had evidently not been designed with wheelchairs in mind. I'd been relieved of my rather attractive drain bag for this outing as well as the morphine drip, so the pain relief was beginning to dwindle. Jay parked me up next to a bench with a shelter and I passed him a pen and my notebook, we needed to write down our questions. At first, they came easily but there was a big one looming over us both about prognosis. The more I tried to put my fears into words the harder it became. Jay held me as I cried, how do you ask the question *'Will I survive this?'* Our moment together was cut short by a thick nicotine fog, the shelter was for smokers and it must have been break time as it was soon busy with staff getting their fix. It was impossible to continue our conversation with a heated debate on sluice duty carrying on beside us. Escape was nice while it lasted and that time together was precious, but we headed back to the café to complete our list.

Back on the ward Audrey bought me some sandwiches saved from the lunch round. Jay had to go, he'd have an evening off visiting now, the driving back and forth wasn't easy. When the evening visitors filtered in, I closed my eyes, listening to the murmur of chatter around me. Betty had a couple sitting with her and Muriel's son had arrived. I tried not to smile as I heard Betty whisper so loudly the bay next door would pick it up, "She's got the cancer you know." Accompanied by heavy sighs and aah's from the relations.

Later I text the girls and Jay goodnight, I was also missing my dogs. What would they be thinking? I walked them every morning, they must be missing me. My drain bag had been removed as the bleed had stopped. The morphine drip remained but the pain was gradually easing, although it felt uncomfortable. Maybe psychologically I could feel the lump I was carrying around, the tumour that had accompanied me silently for so long. I'd been told that tomorrow they would take the catheter out and I was actually looking forward to going for a wee, small pleasures. I settled down to sleep and sleep I did, almost all through the night, in no small part thanks to Audrey and her kind intervention.

CHAPTER 13 DAY 6 QUESTIONS ANSWERED

Day six dawned and I was ready and waiting with my list when the registrar appeared. I had doubted his arrival on the ward after seeing him dressed for the St Patrick's Parade the day before. He was either a moderate drinker or had a strong constitution. The shame was that Jay couldn't be with me; the consolation being that he had helped construct the list I held before me in his handwriting. Was there still a possibility the diagnosis wasn't correct? I was about to find out.

After checking my notes, he came round to the side of my bed.

"Have you prepared your questions then?" I showed him the lengthy list and his eyes widened. "Right so, let's cut to the chase, I suppose you'll be wanting the answers now?" I nodded; my pen was poised ready.

Rather than transcribe the entire dialogue I thought it easier to print my questions together with the answers I scribbled. I don't want to spoil the ending here, but I've also included what actually transpired as you will see; things don't always go according to plan...

Q. When will I have the operation?

A. Three to four weeks.

The surgery actually took place nine days later. I was told it would have been immediately after embolisation as a rule, but the surgeon had been away and was catching up with his list.

Q. What are you removing, what is the cause and how do you know?

A. Cancer. We know a dirty big tumour when we see one.

I think that's what he meant by cutting to the chase. No cause given.

Q. What will be the procedure?

A. Keyhole or open, the surgery will depend upon the size of the kidney as it will have swollen due to the cancer bleeding and subsequent embolisation. This can also cause the tumour to stick and therefore be more difficult to remove, hence usually removing sooner rather than later.

It was keyhole – for a large key.

Q. How long does the operation take?

A. Two to three hours.

Q. Has the CT scan shown full extent of the growth or will the operation be exploratory?

A. Yes. The tumour itself is highlighted well but the surgeon will check the surrounding tissue.

They did a fair bit of digging around apparently.

Q. Will there be a biopsy to determine the grade of the growth?

A. We know what it is.
I didn't get more than this and as you will find out, it was approx. 4 months before I did.
Q. Is there a possibility of recurrence?
A. Always is.
Another succinct answer.
Q. What is the expected duration of my hospital stay post-surgery?
A. Two days.
It was five days, but my notes have me discharged after three.
Q. Explain post op procedure and limitations?
A. Six weeks no chemotherapy or radiotherapy if confined to the kidney.
That's all I wrote – my limitations seemed limitless.
Q. Referral or revue venue post op?
No answer. What I'd meant was please can it be anywhere other than here.
Q. Operation venue?
A. Central, Birmingham.
Q. Will my husband get a chance to speak to the doctor/consultant?
A. If he's here early morning or late evening.
Shame that didn't fit with visiting times...

Well, that's it. All I needed to know about kidney cancer given in a ward round visit on day six of my hospital admission, once again alone.

I was, however, grateful to know what I was facing and felt a little more prepared now.

What I wasn't prepared for was my next visitor, a nurse popped her head into the bay and loudly announced she'd be over to see me in five minutes to remove my catheter. This produced a chorus of 'Oohs' from the resident double act, Muriel and Betty followed by Betty's keen observation.

"A lady I was next to in the other ward told me she had an organism when they took 'ers out."

I'm not sure what was more shocking, Betty's mispronunciation or the revelation. I made sure the curtains were pulled tight before that procedure took place – and no it didn't!

That evening I was able to relay the conversation I'd had with the registrar to Jay. We went through the answers together, there wasn't much more to add. This dirty big tumour was coming out.

CHAPTER 14 27/03/13 THE EVICTION

Following my Q&A session that morning I was told that pending blood tests I may be able to go home later that day. I was feeling rough and very tired but the thought of going home was wonderful despite the knowledge I'd be back soon. I asked one of the nurses on ward duty that morning if I should phone my husband but she said that a doctor would need to see me first and that wouldn't be until later in the afternoon. It would be at least evening visiting time before I'd be able to leave, if at all.

Lunch came and went. I'd most certainly have lost some weight by the time I left here as I'd completely lost my appetite. I was now able to get to the toilet myself; there was a surprising amount of pleasure to be gained from being able to wee again. However, I was still nervous that the bleed may start once more. My only accessory now was the cannula in my hand which still fed pain relief through. Soon after lunch I fell asleep.

I was woken from what must have been a deep sleep by a sharp pain in my hand and I could hear someone saying my name. As I came round there was a Health Care Assistant on one side removing my things from the cabinet and throwing them on the bed. Standing over me was a nurse who was removing the cannula (hence the pain). Still half asleep I asked what they were doing.

"You're being taken down to the discharge lounge." The nurse was now taping a wad of cotton wool over the back of my hand where the canula had been. The HCA meanwhile gathered the get-well cards from the top of the cupboard and was shoving them into a carrier bag with the rest of my belongings. I was totally confused and my tears were coming.

The bedclothes were pulled back as they manoeuvred my legs from under the covers and the HCA rooted around in the carrier, pulling out the trousers I'd arrived in.

"Nobody told me." I stuttered. "My husband doesn't know."

"You'll be able to call him from the discharge lounge." The nurse carefully avoided eye contact and continued trying to feed my legs into the Gwen Stefani trousers – now I knew that wasn't going to be easy!

By now the other patients on the ward were sitting up watching the proceedings looking bemused.

"You can't do that to 'er!" Betty, opposite was waving her arms frantically, "I'll report you."

Muriel soon joined in. "I've heard about this sort of thing but never thought I'd see the day it'd happen in front of my eyes; you should be ashamed."

Much as I appreciated my octogenarian back up it only served to heighten my anxiety, this really shouldn't be happening but what could I do?

Out of nowhere a slightly built man in a smart three-piece suit appeared. His mere presence stopped my renal ward bailiffs in their tracks. For a tense, few seconds the ward stood still as though in some bizarre game of musical statues minus the party tunes. Then, without words the nurse and the HCA slunk back from the bed as this well-dressed mystery man fixed them with an icy stare. He then held out his hand and introduced himself.

"My name is Mr Richards, I'll be performing the surgery to remove your kidney and its tumour."

Bloody hell!

My head was a mess. I'd hardly slept in days, the pain I felt was still biting into my back and side and the canula feeding through pain killers had now been removed. I'd fallen asleep after dinner and woken up to an eviction and now Mr Tweed Suit here was offering his services to open me up.

"Are you ok, is it the morphine?" He looked me up and down.

Tears are streaming down my face; I have a pair of designer trousers hanging off my feet and the bed looks like something Tracey Emin would be proud of.

I pointed at the bed bailiffs, now hovering behind the curtain. "They woke me and started pulling me out of my bed. They've taken the canula out and said I've got to go home?"

"It's a bleedin' disgrace is what it is." Betty was back in defence.

"We all saw it." My other back up Muriel had slid across the dividing curtain with her stick and was pointing it at the nurse and HCA, who had also started crying.

Turning to them himself, Mr Richards instructed; "This lady will not be going anywhere", and by way of dismissal, "I'll speak to you later."

The surgeon then went on to explain he'd been on holiday and as he now had a list to follow my operation wouldn't take place for 10 days. He said normally after an embolisation they would remove the organ as soon as possible but unfortunately this couldn't be the case. He told me that due to the embolisation the kidney would be swollen and may stick (not sure what to?) and so surgery could take longer and dependent upon what they found may be open surgery although keyhole was planned. The game Operation played in my mind with my swollen kidney sounding the buzzer repeatedly as they attempted squeezing it out of my breadbasket.

All this information was being given following the rudest awakening I'd ever had and so I was understandably distressed. As the surgeon left, he went to speak to the Senior Sister, presumably about my treatment as he was not happy.

I took myself off to the toilets and for the first time since arriving at the hospital sobbed and sobbed. Looking back, I think that the seriousness of my condition had just hit me full on but it was not helped by the rude and thoughtless nature by which I was being evicted from my hospital bed.

When I returned to the ward the other patients were also visibly upset and I was beckoned to sit on the bed of a lady who, until now had been noticeably quiet. She whispered to me.

"I train nurses, I didn't want them to know," then nodding towards the nursing staff, "I will have to say something now though."

The mother of a young girl in the bed opposite came over to me.

"I've only ever seen this kind of thing on TV documentaries, they need a hidden camera in here."

This was all so overwhelming; I didn't know what to do. It was going to cause difficulties for the ward staff, would they blame me?

At this point the nurse who had woken me came back in along with the ward matron.

"Come on let's get you back into bed", Standing beside me the nurse took my arm and led me back to my chaotic bed. "I'll draw these curtains, give us some privacy."

"Oh no you won't." Betty's cage was rattled again. "We all saw what happened so we can all hear what you have to say."

The curtains remained open and the matron took a deep breath.

The ward manager then arrived along with the HCA who had taken part in my eviction. The nurse began.

"I don't think you understood us, we weren't making you leave."

That was it, the lady who trained nurses then joined in.

"Yes, you were, we all saw it." With that the mother opposite joined in, agreeing that the staff were worried I'd complain and were desperately trying to cover their tracks.

I assured them I was fully aware of what had happened but that I had no intention of complaining.

What's the point, it wasn't going to change my situation? I could see the HCA was genuinely upset and knew she was only following orders as was the nurse. I understood the pressures placed upon them and the need for beds, what they did to me wasn't personal it was merely badly handled. I'd get over it.

Following this I was visited by two other senior nurses who both asked if I was ok and if I had any complaints. The truth was that if the surgeon hadn't arrived, I would have been sitting in the discharge lounge waiting for my husband to collect me. My mind was made up, I wouldn't be making a complaint, I had enough to worry about.

Later that evening my bloods came back ok so when Jay arrived at visiting time, he could take me home. Leaving the others in the bay was emotional; it's amazing how quickly bonds can form in these situations. I exchanged numbers with the lady who trained nurses whose name I discovered was Jane. A senior nurse herself, she was interested to hear my progress and asked to keep in touch.

As my homecoming hadn't been planned, I travelled back in the clothes I'd arrived in, the Gwen Stefani's were out again and heading home.

CHAPTER 15 DAYS 7-14 LIMBO

I can remember as a child returning from holidays; watching from the car window as we approached home and feeling as though we'd been away much longer. Everything looks familiar but not the same. This is how I felt as we arrived back in Tamworth. It was as if I'd been on another planet, nothing had changed but I had.

Once we were in the house the dogs were alerted to my return. The stairgate, preventing them from running in from the kitchen only just held when they saw me. Both began jumping up frantically, they'd obviously missed me too. We couldn't let them in in case they jumped on me, so I walked carefully to greet them, holding their faces in turn. I told them I was so sorry I'd had to leave them and that we'd be out again soon (wishful thinking).

That first night back I was troubled with weird dreams. Waking up I wasn't sure where I was. I had painkillers for the discomfort in my side, although it wasn't anything like the pain I'd experienced to begin with. The worry was that the bleed would start again so I was told in no uncertain terms to take it easy and do as little as possible until the day of my surgery. There was no chance I'd risk having to go back sooner.

Each morning that week, Jay would bring me a drink and breakfast in bed before leaving for work. When I made my way downstairs later, I'd find my lunch prepared in the fridge. Ruby was back on a day shift but would help her Dad prepare dinner every evening and I was under strict instructions not to do any housework, they had everything under control.

The problem I had that no one else could deal with was my business commitments. That first morning back Joey had a day off and so, together with my Mom helped go through orders that needed posting. My website had remained live and I'd sold some vintage clothing over the previous few days. They wrapped while I sat and wrote apologetic notes for the delay after which I took the shop offline, it was easier. I deliberated for some time about what to post on my website and settled for a white lie; I would be stocktaking over the next couple of weeks. Well I was taking stock in a way.

Another issue that troubled me was who I should tell about my impending surgery. By now, most of my close family were aware. Being an only child with only my Mom remaining, this extended to aunts, uncles and cousins; some of whom lived within walking distance of Central Hospital and were surprised they'd not been told sooner. As Jay is one of six, he made sure his Mom, brothers and sisters and their families knew. I struggled deciding which friends to tell and how much to tell them. It was still difficult coming to terms with the C word and it's a pretty big bombshell to drop into conversation. I settled on saying as little as possible on a need-to-know basis. I told my closest friends and those who would find out by default.

One astonishing thing I found out was that one of my Aunties had also been diagnosed with kidney cancer and it was ultimately what she died of. I knew Aunty Janet had cancer and that she was also treated in Central Hospital, but I hadn't realised she'd had kidney cancer. Another revelation was yet to come... I had been aware that my family were not happy with the level of care she had received, on more than one occasion complaints were made. My Uncle had even confronted the consultant himself, not a pleasant encounter by any means. Now the penny had dropped; I was being treated by the same consultant!

The first person I needed to see was Laura, my closest friend. She was working full time so arranging to meet wouldn't be easy. Somehow, she sensed from a brief phone conversation that something was wrong and arranged to pop in one day. I had rehearsed what I would say, I've got to have surgery to remove a lump but they're not quite sure yet what it is. The problem was that Laura not only knows me well but that she's a nurse and could see right through my deception. She held my hands and asked over and over. "Tell me the truth Deb," and she cried as she held me close. I couldn't, I just couldn't so we left it; but she knew. Laura's father had also been diagnosed with kidney cancer and sadly lost his battle only a few years previously. I'd expected Laura's reaction to be this way, our love for each other is unconditional and no matter how I tried to hide it, she felt my fear.

Another close friend I wanted to see was Fiona; we weren't only friends but worked together often. She ran a creative business and had for many years put my hair in dreadlocks. It was Fi who had been texting me on St Patricks Day and from my brief responses had guessed that something wasn't quite right. We saw each other most weeks and made frequent jollies in her Jeep to Birmingham's Rag Market, our 'business trips'. Our relationship was built on fun and creativity. This was going to be especially difficult news to deliver. As Fi was always so busy (like me normally) there was only one day that she could make. I hadn't wanted to tell her the urgency our meeting held on the phone.

The day in question I had also planned another visitor, Sue. We had only lately become friends through our respective businesses, she was an artist. I wouldn't have chosen to tell her, but Sue had kindly asked me to attend a charity night in London with her, in aid of cancer! It was a celebrity filled event and Sue had offered me the ticket thinking I could have picked up some useful contacts for my designs. Because of this generosity I felt I had to let her know the truth. I was also in desperate need of a haircut and Sue had been a hairdresser before turning to art. When I text, she'd offered to come and restyle my sad Mohican mop.

Thankfully Fi arrived first; I really wanted to deliver the news to her alone. I hadn't bargained for her reaction though. Fi was distraught and cried out, "No, No!"

In some ways it gave me an inner strength. Seeing her so upset meant I automatically became the comforter, reassuring and promising her that everything would be ok. *I was going to be ok.*

When Sue arrived and I relayed the same news, her reaction was quite different, she said she'd guessed as much and was firm in the belief that all would be well, encouraging me to stay positive. Sue had lost her Mother to cancer and so spoke about her experience while she cut my hair.

Three quite different friends; all totally different reactions. I was beginning to learn a lot more about cancer and how people deal with the subject. Even so, I had maintained that until the lump was removed, I wasn't convinced it was cancer – still kidding myself.

During the eight days that I was home I continued with the diary I'd started in hospital. It had been a good idea to keep track of what went on during my stay, the treatment and how I felt. I wouldn't have remembered it all otherwise, so much had happened so fast and I was struggling to keep up. There was a whole new medical language to learn and events that I needed to piece together. In hospital, time is hard to grasp, the chronology was hazy but my journal put everything in place (and led to me writing this book).

I continued this diary at home in the same way noting down my sleep patterns, painkiller quantities and appetite. Also included were the day-to-day occurrences amongst which were Ruby's 21st birthday, not the celebration that we'd had planned as you can imagine. I should have been out preparing beforehand, buying last minute gifts and making sure her day was the most special ever. This all fell to Jay, Joey, Tom and Kevin, Ruby's boyfriend. It was whilst I continued noting down what was happening that it occurred to me to put the diary in blog format. I already had a blog associated with my website so was used to projecting my business life to a wider audience. These notes however were extremely personal and may not transcribe well. Doubts still flooded in so I kept my health scare on a need-to-know basis, writing the journal but keeping it to myself for the time being.

There were several loose ends to tie up before I returned for my surgery. Pending orders had now been posted and the shop remained offline for the time being, but my hypothetical stock take could not go on indefinitely. Running a creative business involves more than making and selling. To sell I had to maintain a vibrant online presence. Everyone was a potential customer which in turn, meant my social media feeds were a constant stream of what I was making, wearing and doing. My creative life in words and pictures filtered throughout Twitter, Instagram and Facebook. Like so many of my peers in creative industries this social media existence is a mirage, a fabulous array of pictures showing off successful businesses whilst making sure to crop out reality. I laughed often about my 'Design Studio' which is really the front bedroom. Although it is a functional workroom (there isn't any bedroom furniture in there) image is everything so to all intents and purposes I could have been situated in a modern studio alongside other creative, hipster types. The reality isn't as glamourous but does mean I can wander in wearing my pyjamas at any time of day or night.

This mock reality meant that I could manipulate the situation I was in so that my customers didn't see me looking this way. Good job as, after dreads and Mohicans, my new cropped haircut didn't make me feel any better, I felt I looked less cute pixie and more post chemo. The fact I was spending my days in loose fitting clothing that didn't press on my swollen kidney and its sinister passenger didn't help and make-up simply wasn't worth it. I didn't have the energy or inclination to continue with any kind of online presence. If I looked like this now, what on earth would I look like post-surgery? It was all too much effort and I could see only one solution, to close my business indefinitely.

In hindsight this was a mistake, one that I regret. What I did next surprises me still and goes to show my state of mind at that time. I was terrified! I needed to be in control and the business was something I couldn't keep control of without telling people the truth. The truth was, I didn't know how this was going to end and so I pushed the button that would take away part of that worry.

I phoned HMRC and explained my situation, I told the advisor that I was unable to run my business and therefore I wanted to close it. After this call I logged into my Facebook business page and did the unthinkable, I deleted it, all 3,904 likes. I then logged out of Twitter and Instagram (thankfully I didn't delete them also). Finally, I packed away what I could of my sewing machinery, fabrics and designs so that little was visible of my work life. I physically and mentally cropped the business out of my life, no need for half-truths and filters now. I had more important business to attend to.

A couple of days before the surgery, Jay took me to the District Hospital for the pre op. This was my first trip outside since leaving Central and it was good to be out in the car. The pre op involved answering a list of questions about my general health along with personal info. I also had some blood tests, an ECG and was weighed and measured; apparently, I had the pulse of an eighteen year-old!

The night before surgery I felt sick, probably nerves. My diary entry reads, 'I enjoyed my last supper'. I wasn't brimming with confidence clearly. I thought back over the past few days, the changes I'd already had to make, how my friendships had been affected. This wasn't only about me and my feelings, it had a profound effect on those around me.

My friend Pauline, who has always been more like a sister, on hearing the news immediately offered me one of her kidneys! Then of course there was my family, the girls and Jay also faced the unknown and would be helpless to change the course of events about to play out. One more sleep and I'd say hello to Central again and goodbye to my left kidney and its cancerous tumour. The wait was nearly over.

CHAPTER 16 DAY 15 THORN IN MY SIDE

I had a fretful sleep. I was worried I'd miss the alarm even though I knew Jay wouldn't. He'd booked the day off work and would be driving me to the hospital and then waiting there until I was out of theatre. Apart from being my first operation, there was still uncertainty about what they would find once I was opened up. My head hurt thinking about it.

As I lay watching the minutes tick by, I thought about the suggestion to name my tumour. This was apparently 'a thing' with cancer patients. Some chose humorous names; others went for a person they disliked immensely or simply gave it a persona like; 'The Wee Bastard'. Many went for celebrity names such as Johnny Rotten or Schwarzenegger, but I didn't think mine deserved a moniker especially one with the catch phrase, "I'll be back!"

Once we were up and ready, snow started falling so we left the house earlier than planned. Jay turned on the radio and Thorn in my Side by Annie Lennox was playing; it couldn't have been more appropriate. My tumour may not have a name, but it did have a theme tune!

I was first on the surgeon's list. We followed directions to a sparse, uninviting room with odd chairs around two walls and a line of cubicles, their curtains drawn along another. Every chair and cubicle were occupied and so we hovered near the doorway until a nurse came across to ask my name. The nurse led us through to a smaller room where she asked a series of questions, one of which was.

"Which kidney is being removed?" I had hoped they would have this important piece of information! I was also handed a hospital gown and instructed to put it on with the front opening, Gulp! There was also a rather fetching pair of surgical stockings which felt as though they'd been made for a Barbie doll. The nurse left while I got changed; there was no cubicle or anywhere to put my clothes. Neither were there any blinds at the window and despite being a few floors up, we were overlooked by several other windows. Jay helped me into the gown, it was bloody cold as well and I felt so uncomfortable.

The nurse returned to do a series of routine tests before we were joined by an anaesthetist who ran through more questions. It was then that the surgeon came in. This would be the first time Jay had met him or indeed any of the doctors whose care I'd been under. My preconceptions of hospital procedure where family members are taken to one side by a doctor and updated on the patients' condition had been dashed early on. There had been a distinct lack of communication and the personal touch hadn't been anywhere near me or my tumour.

The surgeon was a slightly built, middle aged man. He wore a smart three-piece suit in a pale tweed and spoke very softly. He pulled back a chair to sit opposite me; there were only two so Jay stood by my side. The room was so small our knees almost touched. As he sat and began arranging paperwork on his knees, I noticed his small, delicate hands; good sign I thought until he dropped the papers and apologetically scooped them from around my feet. *Hmm, butter fingers, not so good.*

After running through another similar set of Q&As to the ones I'd already answered, he produced a small marker pen and asked me to open my gown and stand. He then proceeded to mark out the entry points on my torso, a kind of treasure map along my stomach and up around to my back. We were then asked if we had any questions. Not having had a biopsy I wanted to know how long before results would be in. Four to six weeks was the reply which seemed an eternity. He informed us that the surgery would take approximately two and a half hours and that I would be in hospital for about three days afterwards.

Time seemed to be on fast forward now and when he said the words,

"See you in theatre," the reality finally hit home.

We were sent to sit out in a wide corridor, me in my gown and stockings and Jay carrying my bag and clothes over his arm. It was eerily quiet and there appeared to be no one about until a nurse appeared dressed in surgical scrubs.

"Debbie?" I nodded. "Would you like to follow me?" She turned and began walking away.

Jay took my hands and kissed me, "I'll see you later."

I couldn't speak, nodding I stood to follow the nurse, tears were rolling down my cheeks. I turned only once to look back at Jay, he looked so lost.

I turned away and with a deep breath followed through the swing doors marked Surgeries.

My first stop was a small admin type room where the nurse in scrubs asked me yet more questions of which included my favourite.

"Which kidney are we removing?" *Should I be worrying?* From there I was taken to a room immediately outside the main theatre where another surgical nurse asked, you guessed it.

"Which of your kidneys are we removing today?" Thank God it wasn't my leg they were taking off!

Next came the weirdest experience of all, I was walked through into the operating theatre. Not so strange you'd think as that's where they would be doing the business but, I had imagined entering this room on a stretcher not on foot. It felt bizarre. As I went in, I was aware of several people in scrubs busy sorting instruments, fiddling with equipment, reading notes. As I made eye contact, they would smile, nod, greet me as though I'd walked into my local for a pint, not entered a high-tech environment ready to go under the knife.

"If you'd like to remove your trainers and climb up onto the bed." It was the anaesthetist I'd met earlier. I obeyed and lay down as if I were about to go for a nap. Well in odd way I was. He then spent some time admiring my sleeve tattoo asking when and where it was done.

"It's too good to pierce," he said, "I'll go in the other side."

As he began inserting the canular the rest of the team swooped in around me and I was positioned and hooked up to various machinery. I lay motionless as they spoke and busied themselves and then the doors swung open and in came the consultant in his surgical gown and gloves. I watched as masks were pulled up and lights were brought over me. For one moment I feared they'd forgotten to put me to sleep and then I was gone.

No countdown, no warning, no dramatic build up or soap style climax. The light simply went out.

CHAPTER 17 PAUSE & REWIND

Less than three weeks before I collapsed and was diagnosed with kidney cancer, I was featured in a business editorial in the local paper.

InsideBusine

She created her own look as a teen. Now

Debbie's clothes are in demand

If the cap fits...

Looking back at the photographs it's strange to think I had a tumour growing inside my kidney. Only two months prior to that I had exhibited my designs at Clothes Show Live in Birmingham, again with no idea I was unwell let alone had cancer.

However, one week before my collapse I found a lump in my armpit, only a small swelling but it made me stop and think. With my Mom having had breast cancer I decided to be sensible and have it checked. At the health centre a nurse examined me and immediately sent me through to a doctor, not what I was expecting. The doctor had a look but as the swelling had gone down a lot he said it was probably glands and most likely a symptom of something else. He advised me to return in two weeks if the swelling didn't go, ten days later my tumour revealed itself.

The penultimate sentence in my business feature read.

'I make clothes that are neither in nor out of fashion but take their inspiration from music and we intend to be around for a long while yet.'

All the time the cancer grew quietly. As I made my plans, dreamed my ambitions and lived my life it waited silently inside. *Time to come out; I have a lot more living to do.*

CHAPTER 18 DAY 15 JELLY AND MORPHINE

I was aware of light, bright light and voices. I couldn't work out if my eyes were open or closed but I knew I was lying down. As consciousness washed over me, I began to remember; *I'm in hospital, I've had an operation, it hurts. It hurts!* I wanted to open my mouth and tell someone; one of the voices in the room but my mouth was glued together. I couldn't move or see properly.

"Debbie, Debbie," the nurse standing over me came into view gradually. "You've had surgery, it's all over now."

I couldn't answer but as I struggled to communicate, she took some kind of small sponge on a stick and put it to my lips then gently into my mouth.

"Try and swallow, it'll get easier." She repeated this a few times and as the moisture went into my mouth, I was able to attempt a thank you.

"There's someone here to see you, I'll be back in a moment." She left me and returned with Jay.

I'm not sure we made much conversation; I could still barely speak and the pain took my focus, but I was so grateful to see his face. It was the briefest of visits, probably meant only to reassure us both that the other was ok. As the fog in my brain cleared, I saw the image of him sitting alone as I was led into theatre and tears stung. We had rarely been apart in our twenty-five years of marriage but the few hours that I'd been in surgery must have seemed the longest ever. I'd come through it; we'd come through it.

I spent some time in the recovery room while they sorted out my painkilling medication before being taken onto a renal ward. I found myself in another six-bed bay. I was still very drowsy and unsure of the sequence of events for a while. Jay had been allowed to stay at the hospital and once I was installed on the ward, returned to my bedside.

The consultant returned sometime that afternoon and thankfully Jay was with me as I remained in a post-surgery fog. He confirmed that the tumour had been removed whole along with my left kidney and they were able to do so by keyhole surgery. This was a huge relief as open surgery had been discussed, particularly as my tumour had bled so much. The consultant went on to say that they'd had a 'good look around' inside me and hadn't identified anything 'nasty', again, good to hear. This was followed up with, 'however, that isn't conclusive as stray cells could be anywhere.' Not as confidence boosting.

I was in a considerable amount of abdominal pain which was apparently due to the gases which were pumped in to inflate me during surgery. A drip attached to a PCA (Patient Controlled Analgesia) was inserted in my arm; this was a wonderful piece of kit. At the push of a button I could administer my own dose of morphine, heaven. I also had the delights of another catheter.

After Jay left that day, I slept a lot. I felt nauseous and couldn't face eating so was brought a dish of jelly which I attempted with little success. The reason for this was that I was unable to move myself up in the bed. Previous experience of pushing the buzzer taught me that I may have to wait some considerable time for help so I lay with the jelly on my chest dropping more over the sheets than I got in my mouth.

When eventually a nurse came to answer my buzz for help, she removed the jelly and said, "We can't do anything about this," she gestured at the bed. "They should have sent you back in a special surgery bed."

When I probed further, she explained that the bed I was in was a standard ward bed but that post surgery there are others specifically used for patients recovering from operations. Apparently, these were in short supply and clearly none were available when I needed one. The nurse continued as though I was in part to blame for this inconvenience.

"If you could get a relative to bring you in a couple more pillows it would help, we can't run up and down to everyone who needs to sit up, it's all we'd be doing all day."

Bedside manner not a strongpoint on this ward either then.

I text Jay asking to bring in another pillow when he next came in and slipped into a morphine induced sleep. It didn't last long, the pain was excruciating, I was uncomfortable in my 'standard ward bed' and felt cold, not something I had experienced during my previous stay as the wards usually seemed oppressively hot.

I was still wearing a hospital gown, presumably one that I'd been put into after the operation. It occurred to me then that I hadn't actually looked at the scene of the crime. I put my hand down beside my left side and gradually moved it up along my waist. My side felt sore from back to front and top to bottom. Looking down there was nothing to see. Approaching from a different angle I tried peering down the front of my gown, a large white pad was visible where the wound would be. Where my left kidney would have been. Man down.

CHAPTER 19 DAY 16 ON MY FEET

I awoke next day in a lot of pain so the PCA was my new favourite accessory. A nurse came to remove the catheter which I was not sorry to see the back of, so I only had the one line in now and I was not going to let go of that easily.

Breakfast arrived about 6.30am. I was happy to get a cup of coffee and bowl of rice crispies as I hadn't eaten at all the day before, except for the failed jelly attempt. My excitement was short lived though as soon after I'd eaten, I felt extremely sick.

Soon after that the ward rounds began, and I received another visit from the surgeon. He checked my wounds during which I chose to look away and he said there'd be no reason why I couldn't leave hospital in a couple of days. A physiotherapist would be visiting me shortly who he said would assist me to get up and out of bed. This news stirred mixed emotions in me, I desperately wanted to be back home but felt extremely nervous about leaving my bed; however uncomfortable.

Sure enough soon after the consultant left my bedside a young, ponytailed girl appeared beside it. She introduced herself as the physio and casually told me I needed to get out of bed and walk to the window. I wanted to cry.

"Let's start with sitting up," she smiled cheerily. I was sitting up. To be able to eat breakfast, the nurses had unceremoniously pulled me up and propped me against the pillow. Without further ado she removed the pillow from behind me and gestured that I lie back down. I looked at my PCA, but she followed my gaze.

"No need for that just yet", again nodding her smiley face and waving her hand for me to lie down.

Slowly and painfully I scooched my way down the bed and gently eased my head back onto the pillow.

"Now, let's see you raise yourself back up."

Bitch!

I placed my hands either side of me and tentatively began lifting myself, inch by inch, sliding my body up the bed. It was horrendous. I stopped each time I made progress to look at her pleading that this torture stop but she remained nodding and smiling. I'd like to say encouragingly but I think she was devoid of feeling.

When I eventually made it back to a sitting position, I insisted I have a shot of pain relief and she reluctantly agreed.

"Now, let's get you out of that bed. I need you to swing your legs to the side and place your feet on the floor. From there we're going to get you to walk across to the window and back."

Who's we? I glared back at Miss Cheshire Cat as she continued her rehearsed lines. She looked all of eighteen and the white uniform and perfect make up she wore gave the appearance more of a beautician than health worker.

My bed was next to the bay entrance, the window was two beds away, it seemed like a mile. Tentatively I moved first my left leg and then the right over the sheets and gently lowered my feet down. They now hung a couple of inches from the floor. It then dawned on me I had no footwear, in fact I wasn't sure where my clothes were, they must be in the cupboard?

"That's it now, feet on the floor."

Fuck off.

I took a deep breath and slid my bum down so that my toes reached the floor. Every slight movement felt like a knife slicing across my abdomen. Ignoring the light-hearted commentary from my torturer I placed both feet fully down. This would get me home. This was good. Wasn't it?

"Ok, now up you get."

I bet she's one of those beauticians who enjoys tearing wax strips off delicate areas.

I took a deep breath and pushed myself forward to a standing position. My head felt light and I had a wobble but then I was up. Less than twenty-four hours after major surgery I was standing on my own two feet.

"Right, make your way to the window." Smiley was writing my progress on her clipboard, not even glancing in my direction.

Barefooted I began shuffling along the hospital floor, suddenly aware of the audience around me. I hadn't paid much attention to the other residents of this bay since my arrival. Now I caught the eye of the lady opposite me who winced as I hobbled forward. I felt sick, it was as though my insides were about to drop straight through me. Every movement along the way hurt, bad, I clutched at the end of my bed until I reached its end. The gap between this and the next bed seemed enormous. Inch by inch I advanced until the windowsill was in reach, I grabbed it with both hands. Turning I noticed the woman in the end bed had a PCA, I wondered would she share but her eyes were closed?

"Well Done!" Smiley did that ridiculous palm, clappy hand thing in mock admiration of my feat. "Back you come." Taking a deep breath, I took a step forward and the world went into spin drive.

Next thing I knew I'm stretched across the end of the bed next to the window, its occupant still seemingly asleep. The physio had sprung into action and was now leaning over me coaxing, in a far gentler manner that I try and get back up. From there she let me lean against her as I limped back to bed painfully. I felt as though I'd been assaulted, everything hurt, including my pride.

Whilst I fully understand the importance of getting patients out of bed at the soonest opportunity after surgery, surely a little common sense should be brought into play. If someone tells you it hurts too much, then it probably does. I suppose the physio was only 'doing her job', the same as everyone else in that hospital machine was. There were boxes to tick and judging by Smiley's clipboard she'd got a full house with me.

Despite this unpleasant experience I felt the day to have been a positive one. Later that evening I got myself out of bed again and managed the walk to the bathroom which felt liberating. Had I not been 'encouraged' earlier that day I may not have felt capable. For the first day post-surgery it was a big step forward to getting me back home.

CHAPTER 20 DAY 17 HEARTACHE

I don't think I slept at all that night; it was hard to get comfortable. They still hadn't managed to get a suitable bed, so I remained on the flat trolley type cot and the pain was bad. Sometime in the early hours I had to buzz for a nurse. Most of the pain was concentrated in my tummy and lower back but I had started to get pains in my chest. Every time I breathed in, I felt there was nowhere for the air to go, it was as though my lungs wouldn't fill up. The nurse on duty was concerned and called for a doctor who attached me to an ECG to monitor my heart. The results were ok and as suspected the pain stemmed from trapped gases that were pumped in during surgery, quite common. The doctor advised that my pain medication be increased; he then noticed that the PCA had run out. I hadn't been receiving any morphine for some time - well that explained a lot.

After finally managing to nod off I was rattled awake again by my bed being moved. Opening my eyes, I found two nurses unhooking the equipment from the wall and wheeling me out of the bay. Once again, along with various other residents I was being relocated due to issues with the mixed ward. Of the four bays, three were generally all men and only one for women. However, two had recently been given over to women but more men had now been admitted. To complicate matters, not all the women were renal patients and had been allocated temporary beds pending spaces in whatever ward they were supposed to be in. It was ridiculous, beds were moving in and out of bays, some out of the ward, others parked in the corridor waiting for a space elsewhere and all in the middle of the night. Sleep would have to wait.

When I eventually reached my new parking slot it was next to a window. The East Birmingham skyline may not be pleasing to the eye, but it lifted my spirits. I watched as vapour trails patterned the grey sky and the occasional bird flew close enough for me to spot. Sitting up I could see corrugated factory roofs and tall chimneys; it was a landscape I was familiar with from childhood days visiting my Nan.

As a new day dawned in my new bay we were introduced to the most entertaining nurse I'd come across. Precious could be heard from the other end of the corridor singing and she danced around our beds whilst updating charts and checking observations. We were all given nicknames by her, mine was Smiler and her demeanour raised spirits after what had been a difficult night.

I was also kept amused by the continual bickering of staff who were understandably annoyed about bed shortages. They blamed other wards for the complaints they now faced; believe me, some patients didn't take the bed move lying down (if you know what I'm saying).

The registrar on the ward round that day said it was time to take me off the morphine, the drip would be removed and I would be on paracetomol and codeine from now. It was good to finally be free of cannulas, much easier to move about but the pain remained the same, bad.

Jay and the girls had been visiting since my surgery, but I'd asked that no one else come. For one thing there were strict rules about how many visitors per bed – not that all people took notice of this. Mostly though I felt unwell and wouldn't be good company. There would be plenty of time once I was home for relatives and friends to call in. However, there were a couple of friends who had wanted to visit and Jay thought seeing them would do me good. We'd known Laura and Thomas over twenty years, meeting when our girls were younger at Irish dance class. We'd shared the best times together and as our respective daughters grew up, our bonds grew stronger.

As Jay was working, his visits were made in the evening, so when Laura and Thomas walked into the ward that afternoon I was pleasantly surprised. It was a little emotional; both being nurses they weren't strangers to hospitals but seeing me there must've been a shock. Last time we'd all socialised together had been around their kitchen table where the menu would have been Stella Artois and music. Laura had a few tears as we hugged and she told me how she'd known things were worse than I'd let on when visiting me the week before my surgery. I couldn't have told her the truth back then; I knew how she'd take it and didn't want to upset her more.

Thomas had come bearing gifts, he handed me two take away cartons which in other circumstances I would have expected to find curry and rice. Lifting the lids, I found fresh strawberries and grapes. The nursing staff looked relieved!

The visit was over too soon, seeing my friends made me feel more myself again. Hospital can take away your identity. You become a patient on a bed in a bay within a ward, known by your ailment rather than your name or personality. I'd had a glimpse of reality and it was about to get nearer still. The doctor on the evening ward round said that there should be no reason why I couldn't go home the next day. Finally.

CHAPTER 21 DAY 18 HOME TIME

I had another restless night. Does anyone sleep in hospital? The bay was extremely noisy, the woman opposite me was on some class of breathing apparatus that produced a sound something between a snore and water going down a plughole. We were next to the nurse's station, which was busy day and night, conversations were held at full volume regardless of the hour. Another patient had a hacking cough interspersed with prolonged heaving. Only one other lady, apart from me was a renal patient. Bed shortages dictated who went where.

It was Easter Sunday, and I watched a beautiful sunrise over East Birmingham and hoped I'd see the sunset back at home later. With this in mind I carefully eased my legs out of the bed and set to sorting out my things in the cupboard. In the absence of more suitable trousers I had arrived in the Gwen Stefani's. I folded my clothes and placed them on top of my bag, so I'd be ready to leave as soon as I was able.

That morning's ward round was far more relaxed, as it was a holiday quite a few regular staff were away. The doctor that came to see me was a locum, he was dressed in surgical scrubs and I'm not sure what his specialism was, but I liked him as soon as he spoke.

"You need to go home," he smiled, "it's so noisy in here you can't possibly have slept." Then by way of an afterthought, "And the food is terrible!"

He said I needed rest and to eat properly and the best place for that was home. I couldn't agree more.

A little while later I had some routine blood tests and a nurse came to chat about wound care which was mainly 'Don't touch it or get it wet.' I was also instructed on how to inject Clexane, a blood thinning drug that would prevent post-surgery clots. This came in measured syringe doses and had to be injected directly into my stomach for the next twenty-eight days. Puncturing my tummy with a needle didn't faze me too much when the reward was going home to my own bed.

As I was expecting to leave later that day, I skipped lunch, there's only so much cheese pie anyone can take and the one on their menu didn't appear to contain cheese. Jay arrived early afternoon and waited with me as the day dragged on and on. By dinner time there were still no drugs. We decided to leave with a part prescription, Jay would return the following day to collect what remained. Ridiculous really when we could have been given a prescription to collect from a local chemist. Once again, a wheelchair was scrounged, and Jay pushed me back out of the hospital and over to the car.

It was a painful drive home; abdominal surgery certainly highlights every pothole and bump in the road. No matter how carefully J drove there was no escaping the jolts.

**One of the most useful tips I've heard since is to have a pillow with you for your journey home after abdominal surgery. Place it over your wound and under the seatbelt. Hindsight is a great thing!*

We parked in the side road by our house and I waited for Jay to come round and help me out of the seat. Standing on the pavement while he grabbed my bags from the boot, one of the neighbours approached me and as he went by tapped my side saying, "Evening." I nearly collapsed on the spot. He wasn't to know I was fresh off a hospital ward with an extremely tender wound but what are the chances?!

It was another tearful reunion with my dogs although I couldn't let them near me in case they knocked my wound. Ruby had made pizza and I managed to sit long enough to eat it on the sofa, which I hadn't realised was so low until now. Getting up again was not easy.

Climbing into my own bed was heavenly after the hard hospital mattress, memory foam never felt as good. The only issue I had was the weight of the continental quilt, just about anything that touched the area of my wound hurt like crazy. I had to lift my knees up to make a tent for the covers to avoid contact with my side. I slept off and on. I think the realisation of what I'd been through hit home. I was back minus a kidney; my life had altered for good.

The following day Jay rang the hospital to be told the drugs were still not available, it would be later that evening before he could collect them. The Clexane prescription was not something I was keen to experiment with and over the next days and weeks I began to dread those daily injections. My tummy became sore and bruised from jabbing them in.

I desperately wanted a shower or a bath, but this was strictly forbidden for three weeks, I couldn't risk getting the wound wet. In its place I had to wash with a flannel, this was impossible at first as I couldn't bend and twist, so the girls stepped in to help, my own personal nurses.

By my third day at home I was feeling more unwell and the wound was looking angry. There were three incisions, the largest running diagonally across my tummy to my groin and two smaller, one beside my belly button and another at the same height but in my side. The small wounds were healing ok, these were apparently the 'keyholes' where instruments were poked in to free the kidney. The large diagonal one was where the kidney had been taken out. This now had a huge slug like blister running alongside it filled with something disgusting. Both daughters were unhappy with the state of it and arranged for a District Nurse to come out. What's surprising is that, had the call not been made, no provision for wound care from a professional had been advised. For that matter I hadn't received anything conclusive to say what I'd been through. At that time there were no forthcoming appointments or even nurse clinics set up. I was told to wait and something would arrive in the post. On leaving hospital I was handed a discharge sheet which read.

Main diagnosis: Left laparoscopic nephrectomy. Findings + Treatment: Pt had left nephrectomy.

Pt recovered well post op with no complications.

Pt c/o pain after operation but this settled with simple analgesia.

She was sent home on analgesia with clexane for a total of twenty-eight days.

Out Pt follow up 3/52

The statement that my pain had settled with simple analgesia was false as I'd had the morphine via the PCA. The only reason I came home was I'd either starve or go mad with sleep deprivation if I stayed, the pain was real. The information that my outpatients follow up would be in three months was frightening because there was nothing else in place. I'd not seen a specialist nurse or anyone to discuss the cancer as I was on a renal ward. The Macmillan nurses didn't come near which had been the case when my Mom was diagnosed with breast cancer. I hadn't seen any literature either on kidney cancer or any other for that matter. The whole experience had been like a fog, it happened but I wasn't sure how or why.

CHAPTER 22 10 DAYS POST SURGERY

The District Nurse arrived the following morning, a motherly lady around the same age as me who I warmed to immediately. She was genuinely concerned when she saw the state of my wound and its slug.

"There's not really a lot I can do with that but re-dress it, I can't believe you've been discharged without care?" Her question resonated with me, should I have phoned sooner, was there an appointment I'd missed? As she worked gently, cleaning around the wounds across my abdomen she asked more about my surgery.

"Have you received biopsy results; did they explain how the surgery went?"

I told her what I knew which was that it had been successful. I remembered the surgeon said he'd had a 'good look around and not identified anything else nasty.'

"Yes, but did he explain how that was carried out?" I considered this; it was something I had wondered but at the time hadn't pressed him on. The consultants are so busy, their time so precious I hadn't thought it right to question him further on the 'ins and outs' of my operation. I shook my head.

"Well, for a start you wouldn't have been lying flat for the duration of the surgery." The nurse sat back on a stool facing me after completing my wound care. "They would have twisted and turned you. Those smaller scars are incisions made for the instruments used to release the organ they are removing. The kidney itself comes out of the bigger hole here." She pointed at the slug wound. "Your left leg was probably moved across the right." Demonstrating she crossed her legs and leaned over. "You see? How else would they get the kidney from up here to down there?" I nodded; it was beginning to make sense. Also explained the odd bruises I'd found. "Then you have to consider how they get such a large kidney; bearing in mind it was carrying a tumour, past all the other bits and pieces?" She raised her eyebrows; I had not expected an anatomy class. "Well, they have to move them out of the way first." My turn to raise eyebrows. "There's also all that muscle, fat and tissue to get through," she went on. "Not to mention manoeuvring the kidney out of that hole?" At this the game Operation came to mind again...

"I'm no expert of course, but I do think you should hear these details from the person who performed the surgery. It helps to understand the procedure and after all, it's your kidney they removed, you have a right to know."

Yes, I nodded. I do want to know; I did want to know but I didn't know how to ask. Everything happened so fast. Hospital was an alien place, unwelcoming and harsh. I hadn't wanted to get it wrong, hadn't known what was right.

"If you don't ask you don't get unfortunately." As if reading my mind, she carried on, "Hospital can make mutes of us, you feel afraid to question, you feel they're the experts so just let them do their job. You deserve to know exactly how your surgery went; it's taken a vital part of you away."

The nurse got up and began packing away her things. She must have spent at least half an hour with me.

"Don't hesitate to call if you're at all worried, one of us will come out and check that wound again if it doesn't improve." As she picked up her bag and coat, she leaned into me, taking my hand.

"Don't be afraid to ask questions. I'll let myself out."

Alone again I reached for my diary and began writing all those unanswered queries that had been racing around my head. She was right, they had been there all along I was simply afraid to ask, maybe afraid of the answers. I was right about one thing though; I really should not have been left high and dry after being discharged.

Despite this, I was fortunate to have my own personal nurses in the girls and Jay was looking after me incredibly well. I was finding it difficult not being able to do normal things for myself. Things I would take for granted like walking the dogs, changing the bed, shopping and making dinner all seemed out of reach. Personal care was the real struggle though, especially not being able to take a bath. I had to give it a go but knew Jay and the girls were keeping a close eye on me, so I waited until they were all at work.

I felt like a naughty child running the bath. I only filled it about three inches and didn't put any bubble bath in. With a towel close at hand I carefully lifted one leg over the side of the bath, not too bad. Clutching the side, I took the weight off my other leg and swung it over, ouch! Catching my breath, I then slowly, painstakingly knelt into the water, bliss. Undeterred by the pain I washed cautiously, keeping away from the site of my surgery, it was heavenly to feel water again. Trying to get out however was more like hell. Gripping the bath sides, I attempted to lift but couldn't move for the agony. I stopped to assess my situation. Alone, naked in the bath with the door locked and unable to move. What was I thinking of? I had to get out, if only to avoid getting in trouble with my family. This had been a bad move. Every motion I made was a bad move right then! Steeling myself I held tight and gradually raised myself up to standing then gingerly managed to get my legs back out onto the bathmat. Sitting on the bath side wrapped in a towel I cried tears of relief (and pain). I would do as I was told from now on.

CHAPTER 23 REVELATIONS

I had stopped writing in my hospital notebook regularly, there wasn't really much to say but I was filling in my diary. The days stretched out before me, but I couldn't do much at all, there was little to report. I'd not reactivated any of my social media feeds. It was hard enough feeling physically ill without the mental anxiety of worrying about the jobs I was losing. I had worked so hard to build my business but still couldn't see a way of explaining why I'd dropped off the face of the planet. In my head, fashion and cancer did not mix. I imagined it would be off putting. My designs were fun and funky, currently those words had vanished from my vocabulary. The cliché of being 'a shadow of your former self' was an apt description. My hair was cropped short, make up wasn't a consideration; not that I had ever bothered much. I had often ridiculed another cliché when people say they're 'trying to find themselves' in whatever context it's used. At that moment though, I had no idea who I was. Was I still a fashion designer? Was I a cancer patient now the tumour had been removed? The reflection in the mirror looked nothing like the me of a few of weeks ago.

Choosing clothes was a real issue and I was spending most of my time in dungarees, so it was time to bite the bullet and invest in a loose-fitting jogging suit. ASOS was at that time my go-to place to shop online. I had my own boutique on the site although it was currently closed. I'd been so proud to open it, one of the first boutiques to open on ASOS Marketplace. ASOS had opened its Marketplace platform a couple of years before, allowing independent designers to trade from virtual market stalls across the world. I'd been lucky enough to qualify early on, back when being accepted for a boutique was still prestigious, I was boutique number 43. There are currently over 800 and the criteria for gaining one has dropped – as has the prestige (and quality).

My look until that point had been eclectic to say the least. I was no shrinking violet. Now though I wanted comfort and drawing attention was not on my agenda. My resulting purchase was not altogether sensible as it was printed in Disney's Fantasia design so resembled pyjamas. A hint I wasn't ready to conform just yet.

I had also lost nearly a stone in weight! I'm fairly sure it wasn't all kidney and had more to do with hospital diet, but the result was ill fitting clothes. As I was unable to fasten the waistband of jeans it meant things were literally falling off me.

I was taking more interest in my diet than I had ever done previously. Being naturally slim I had never been over 9 stone in weight, hovering around 8 and a half most of my adult life. I'd always been able to eat and drink pretty much anything which included sugar, salt and alcohol. Now I wanted to know more about what I consumed and whether it was good for me and my lone kidney.

Housework was more challenging; despite Jay and the girl's insistence that I leave jobs for them I found it hard to ignore things during the day. Hanging the washing out for instance meant reaching up with only my right hand as stretching my left side was too painful. I developed a method of throwing clothes up then hooking/pegging quickly. Changing the bed was another mammoth task and dragging Henry hoover around became a real chore. It is hard to believe how debilitating abdominal surgery is, weeks became months and I was still struggling with the most mundane physical tasks.

Sleep had never been a problem for me in the past and apart from the initial pain I experience post-surgery, I was still able to get a decent night's sleep. It was some time before I was able to lie on my left side and even on my back I tended to put my knees up so the covers didn't sit on my wound, but I slept relatively well. The only difference was strange dreams, quite unlike anything I had experienced before.

I was receiving a few visitors, mainly family and the few close friends who I had let into my secret circle. I realised it was getting awkward for them to fob people off when asked about where I'd disappeared to. It was time to 'come out', admit to others – and myself, I've had cancer.

Funnily enough it was the window cleaner who was next to know. He called to collect his money and Ruby answered the door, I heard the conversation.

"Hi, is your Mom in?"

"Erm, yes but she's not well enough to come to the door."

"Oh no, what's wrong?"

"She's had cancer."

"What?!"

"Kidney cancer, she's had surgery to remove it."

"The cancer?"

"Yes, and her kidney."

"The. Whole. Kidney!"

The shock in his voice made me laugh out loud. It sounded so ridiculous. To be fair I would not have had a clue how big a kidney was and had never heard of kidney cancer before this. I could see my news was going to be a shocker.

I relented and agreed that my illness could be made more public but would hold off social media a bit longer. I wasn't feeling up to answering too many questions yet, it was probably just as well.

CHAPTER 24 3 CANULAS, 2 X-RAYS & a CT SCAN

Two weeks go by without an entry in my journal until this.

The past couple of days have not felt good, the pain isn't easing, and my back is especially sore. The thing bothering me most is shortness of breath. Even climbing the stairs leaves me feeling faint and tired.

The District Nurse returned to check my wound. She took a swab as she thought it looked infected but was especially concerned about my breathlessness and made a doctor's appointment for me that day.

I already had an appointment later in the week to see the GP with Jay. Being told I had to go sooner upset me because I worried I would hear more news on my own. Jay had to be with me this time. The nurse assured me she would relay this to the GP and nothing about my cancer diagnosis or the biopsy would be discussed but I needed to be seen that day.

Soon after, Ruby drove me down to the surgery where I was seen by a female doctor. She examined me then began making a call.

"You need to go straight back to hospital." As this bombshell sunk in the GP spoke to the Emergency Department at the District Hospital telling them to expect me.

"Can you make your own way, or shall I arrange an ambulance?"

An ambulance? This was moving way too fast. I turned to Ruby who confirmed she would be able to run me to the hospital.

The doctor stood up, our cue to move.

"You need to go directly to A&E, take this." She printed out a sheet, putting it in an envelope and handing it to me. "I'm sure everything will be fine but there's a possibility you have a blood clot, you need to go right away."

And that was it. Off again.

Reaching the Emergency Department, I gave my name to the receptionist. When we were seated, I realised I still had the envelope the doctor gave me. It wouldn't harm to look. The information appeared to be my medical history, which was brief, two pregnancies and then the nephrectomy. It was what was typed above these details that puzzled me though.

Pyelogram – 1975 – Outcome – Kidney disease.

My mind raced back and forth to the memories of my father's kidney stones and tests that had been carried out on me aged six or seven. Surely this was relevant? Had this been discussed or even acknowledged? What if it was my remaining right kidney that had been weaker? I showed Ruby who was also surprised.

It wasn't long before I was called through and asked to climb up onto a bed. Once again, I was hooked up to monitors and my observations taken by a nurse, my blood pressure was extremely low. When a doctor arrived, I handed him the envelope and he scanned it briefly.

"What does it mean? I've got a history of kidney disease?"

"We need to get a canula in first." Totally ignoring my question, he took hold of my hand and proceeded to insert the canula, I almost leapt off the bed. Having had several such tubes pushed into my veins, never had one hurt quite as much. So much, in fact, that I quite forgot about my line of questioning as the doctor retreated out of the bay. My cannulised hand began to throb and the pain built until it was excruciating. Ruby called a nurse for me who took one look at my swollen wrist and exclaimed, "I'm not sure that was necessary?" Then shaking her head assured me she would be right back. Returning with a junior doctor she pointed out the large tube poking out of my wrist and he agreed it needed changing. Unfortunately, he wasn't a great aim, missed the vein and the drugs (which I was still oblivious about) started tissuing (pumping into tissue rather than vein). Eventually, with much apologising he struck a vein and I was finally administered whatever it was they wanted to pump in. The shock and pain had rendered me stupid again as I didn't have a clue what it was. The nurse lingered only to give me some advice.

"Pink canulars are far easier to insert and much less painful on a small hand like yours so if a doctors approaches with a green, tell them pink's your favourite colour. "

We were alone again for an hour or so before I was taken in a wheelchair for X-rays. The radiographer firstly asked what had happened to my hand which was by now black and blue.

"That looks painful!" He then went on to put the fear of God into me by saying that with only one functioning kidney I should question the decision to send me for another CT scan especially with contrast.

"It has to work far harder to filter the dye around. You want to take care of that one." *You don't say?*

He went on to X-ray me back and front and return me to the A&E bay where Jay had now relieved Ruby and was waiting for me. This had not been planned. He was to spend another five hours waiting there while a bed was found for me. I had been on a trolley for eight and a half hours, no food or drink. My next stop was rather unexpected. I was admitted to the High Dependency Unit.

My bed stood alone in the centre of a fair-sized room that had windows to all sides. One towards the outside world, the others facing onto the ward. Each were covered by venetian type blinds that flicked up periodically as someone peeped in. It was both reassuring and unnerving at the same time. I was brought a plate of biscuits and a hot cocoa and sat up in the bed listening to the sound of machinery and drips clicking and bleeping. *How had I ended up here?*

Throughout the night I was checked up on, so I didn't get much sleep. First thing in the morning I was wheeled off again for a CT scan. I posed the question about the suitability of the dye, given my lone kidney and was reassured it would be fine. After this I was returned to HDU to await my results.

A couple of hours passed and then a pleasant doctor introduced himself, apologised for the wait and gave me the best news, no blood clot, I could go home.

CHAPTER 25 HELPLINE

I could not wait to get back to normal, but it was a new normal post cancer; I simply didn't realise that yet. I was feeling ok in general; my wound was healing well but I still had a nagging pain in my right side. The need to get some closure, hear the result of my surgery was consuming me. An appointment had come through, but it wasn't for 12 weeks and that seemed an eternity.

I'd begun getting out again. Most evenings I would go a walk with Jay and the exercise began making movement easier. The scarring on the left was still sore and the pain in my right side meant I almost limped along. I was developing a very odd gait.

We live close to the town centre, so close I had never needed a car and would walk most places or get the train as the station is also nearby. My first walk into town was strange. For a start I realised how slow I was; normally at a quick step this would take me five minutes. It was exhausting too, every curb stone jolted me, the pain in my back all too evident.

Part way there I had to take a rest, I felt dizzy and even considered turning back. It was ridiculous, I had walked this route most of my life, in all weathers, with pushchairs and prams, worse the wear after a night out and never had I thought it was too far.

It was a beautiful spring day, as I reached the town centre, I noticed the trees had the first blossoms on them. People were milling about, buses were driving back and forth, the market was on and there was a general chatter in the air, I'm sure I could even hear birds singing. I remember standing next to the Co Op in the centre of town and feeling a sense of wonder, it was as if I was seeing everything for the first time and it was bizarrely beautiful. I know that sounds kind of strange, but it was as though I'd been on another planet for months and was returning to earth. I don't think I had ever noticed birds singing in the town centre before, revellers leaving pubs maybe, market traders shouting definitely but not the sights and sounds of nature. It was a morbid kind of wonder. It was all still here, life going on and I needed to appreciate it more.

My sense of euphoria didn't last as I soon became tired and the pain in my back was beginning to gnaw so I resorted to getting the bus home. It was a start though; I could build on that.

I was pleased I'd met no one I knew in town. I still felt uncomfortable telling people what I had been through, unless they asked directly, I preferred not to say. A classic example was my next-door neighbour who I saw frequently but who didn't appear to notice my physical decline. It was six months before we had a conversation in which I revealed I'd had kidney cancer, she was astounded and couldn't believe she hadn't known, but why would she? The only outward sign that anything had changed was that I walked a little slower and more carefully for a while.

I made an appointment with the GP who had advised me about the lump I'd found in my armpit; he would have received notification by now of my surgery and would know more than me. Jay came with me and we had expected to receive news about the biopsy as nothing had arrived from the hospital and the consultant appointment was still a way off. The GP produced a small printout from the hospital which consisted of two sentences saying I'd had my left kidney out, the size and grade of the tumour and the date I was discharged. That was it.

We asked questions about the description given of the tumour size and grade. We needed to know about the chances of it returning or worse, already being present elsewhere. What about life expectancy, how would my remaining kidney cope? There were so many unanswered questions, but the doctor was unable to give the answers saying,

"You need to get this information from your consultant." He was very pleasant and understanding; gave us plenty of time and helped as much as he could but he was unable to give that peace of mind we desperately needed. His parting words were, "Don't Google it."

He did recommend patient.co.uk and said MacMillan Cancer would be good to talk to. There were no leaflets of information on kidney cancer at the GP's surgery but one of those organisations may be able to provide me with something factual. I took his advice in part, but it was hard not to Google. What I really wanted to know was how other people had coped with kidney cancer, real stories, good and bad. I was feeling incredibly isolated. My family and friends couldn't do enough for me, but they could not stop this feeling of dread that lingered. I needed answers.

Google threw me a lifeline as one of the top results directed me to The James Whale Fund for Kidney Cancer. A charity set up by the broadcaster, following his own battle with the disease. As well as information and help sheets that could be sent off for, there were stories from survivors. Finally, I was reading about how other people had been diagnosed and treated, it was a revelation. Part of the site was dedicated to fact sheets and advice; I was learning about the disease that had invaded me. Not in a morbid way, the explanations were concise and gave just enough knowledge for the patient to understand their illness without being more afraid of it. There was also a helpline given with access to trained professionals, someone to talk to who could identify with and allay those fears, give you some perspective. I decided to call.

The lady I spoke to was called Lee. As it was a spur of the moment call, I hadn't rehearsed what so say. I began explaining my rapid descent from fashionista to cancer patient via two ambulances and three hospitals. I mentioned the treatment, my confusion, the lack of information and the state of hopelessness I now felt. Lee listened. I became tearful. I was probably incoherent at times, but it all poured out. I was sitting at the top of the stairs, talking to a stranger and I had an epiphany. I was part of a select group. I was a cancer patient and I needed help. Until then I had merely coped, well actually I had leaned on my family, let things happen around me. I had not actually confronted my cancer. I wasn't really given the opportunity. I spoke to Lee about my feelings of anger. Having cared for my Mom during breast cancer I'd seen the other side of the coin. I'd held her hand when she was diagnosed in a breast care unit by a consultant who was joined by a specialist nurse and a Macmillan nurse. We'd had the leaflets, the helplines, even the dedicated groups for Mom to belong to (she is still a member of Breast Friends). From start to finish her treatment had been second to none and this was my precedent. This was not however my experience. Lee listened.

By the time I put down the phone I felt lighter. Lee couldn't remove the anxieties I harboured but she had helped me face them. During the call she had mentioned writing things down, journaling is a tried and tested way of controlling emotions, decluttering those fearful thoughts and making sense of stressful situations. I told her about my notebook and the blog I wanted to pursue, this was a positive and something Lee encouraged. More than anything I had found my group. Only a few short weeks ago I hadn't even heard of kidney cancer. Over those weeks I'd felt like the only person who had this disease, it was a lonely diagnosis and alien treatment, I was fast becoming reclusive. The James Whale Fund for Kidney Cancer had given me hope and belonging. I had found my new tribe.

CHAPTER 26 BLOG

The chat with Lee made me reconsider the diary I had been writing and my self-imposed isolation. It had helped to share my feelings and reading other patient accounts on the charity's website gave me a sense of relief and belonging. I had been good at social media so why not step back in? What had I got to lose, I was down a kidney and a considerable amount of dignity not to mention confidence? Maybe I could share my experience?

I began researching blogging sites, experimenting with WordPress and Blogger, reading other blogs and getting a feel for how they worked. Previously I had written blogs for my business that were attached to my website or Facebook. This would be a dedicated kidney cancer blog that stood alone; my feelings would be laid bare. I needed to get it right.

I settled on Blogger but then I had an even bigger decision to make. What was I going to call it? I sat with pen and paper writing down various options, from humorous to edgy. Before becoming a cancer patient, I had been a businesswoman, a fashionista. It was ironic then that the type of cancer I would develop was not widely known, one that I'd heard term 'an old man's cancer'. That was it, An Unfashionable Cancer!

I had a platform and now I had a title, all that remained was to share my diary online. The easy part was transferring the contents of my little book to the laptop. Clicking that share button was quite another matter. I had decided to write in retrospect as several weeks had now passed. This way I could drip feed the content slowly until I eventually caught up to date. It wasn't actually that easy copying out my diary, I realised I hadn't re-read the book as I'd gone through. There were parts of it that were still very painful.

I took it offline three times before I kept it live.

By the time my 'story' was out there more of my friends and acquaintances had got to know that I'd had cancer. I figured that if even the window cleaner knew it was about time I braved the Facebook announcement. So it was, that six weeks after I returned from hospital, I posted an update on social media.

Apologies for disappearing off the scene for a while, some of you may not yet know I've been unwell. Back in March I discovered very suddenly that I had kidney cancer, after spending time in hospital I was taken for surgery where they removed both kidney and tumour. Right now, I'm home recovering so I'm afraid the business has to take second place for a while. I was unable to speak about all this as it was happening, hope you understand? Debbie X

Again, it took some time and a lot of courage before I could click the button that made this post live. It is strange that announcing a cancer diagnosis was akin to a confession of some kind. Nothing about it sat comfortably and for a while after I was afraid to check my notifications. Before posting the update, I was not at all curious about what everyone else had been up to either. Prior to my 'disappearance' I would have checked social media updates throughout the day, now I wasn't interested. I had spent long enough in relative isolation with life carrying on around me making no impact at all, why did I need to know the minutia of my acquaintance's daily routines?

Later that day I did check back in and was shocked by what I found, reams of comments. Some brief, thinking of you, sending love content but most heartfelt messages with beautiful words and sentiment. I honestly couldn't believe what I was reading, I had underestimated the depth of feeling people held for me, these weren't only offhand comments, every word meant something. Quite a few referred to my business, one that sticks in my mind was from a fellow designer who'd said he thought I'd been poached by a big design house and would next see my work on the catwalks of Dolce & Gabanna or Versace, that made me smile. I would like to be able to relay more of these comments, but the truth is that only a few short months later I deleted Facebook altogether and they were all lost.

CHAPTER 27 VERDICT

I was told an appointment with the consultant who performed my nephrectomy would be arranged for approximately four weeks post-surgery. The wait for this to drop through the letterbox seemed an eternity. Every morning I would anxiously check the post and as the weeks dragged on my anxiety grew. I needed an answer to the most crucial question I'd ever have to ask. *'Has it spread?'* Despite having been warned of the dangers of Google by my GP, it's hard to resist those searches on sites such as patient.com and healthline.com in fact I pretty much exhausted my options on the world wide web by the time the longed for envelope dropped through my door several weeks after leaving hospital.

During those weeks, I was unable to find reassurance from any other professional. My GP was good but could not allay my fears. The District Nurse had been wonderful but was unable to give me peace of mind.

My blog had begun to gather momentum as I was now sharing the posts on Twitter. This had introduced me to a few more kidney cancer patients. Some had found the blog via the James Whale Fund website. Between us we were able to compare notes as we were at varying stages of the disease.

One of the followers I was introduced to was Judi Bond, she was a similar age to me and had been diagnosed with kidney cancer a couple of years previously. Having also undergone a full nephrectomy, unfortunately her cancer had metastasised elsewhere and she was continuing with treatment. Judi was a runner and despite gruelling immunotherapy, continued to train, even at longer distances, she was truly inspirational. Despite only connecting virtually, I felt a real affinity with her, she was unstoppable with a fighting spirit and upbeat personality. I was finding this was common amongst cancer sufferers, particularly those who forged ahead with physical fitness pursuits where possible.

My existing Twitter followers were also interacting with the kidney cancer blog posts which could be amusing. I had gone from a fashion designer who tweeted about catwalk shows and photoshoots to a recovering cancer patient sharing descriptions of my condition and the care I received? I recall a tweet from a regular follower @midgediabolik stating 'your medical vocabulary has expanded' when I posted about nephrectomies and metastases. That made me smile as the language I was using was certainly not fashionable anymore.

The word metastasis in particular was high on my anxiety radar at that time. In the brief chat I'd had with the consultant the day after surgery he'd said that they'd 'had a good look around my abdomen and nothing had shown up but the biopsy would tell more.'

The hospital appointment was part of a urology clinic. Jay took the day off work to drive me over and when we arrived, the waiting room was full and patients spilled out along the corridor. There was a nurse at a desk outside the consultant's room with a huge pile of cardboard files, she appeared to be sorting them into an order. Occasionally we would catch a glimpse of the consultant as the door to his room opened, even the sight of him filled me with dread. He held the news that could change my life.

After a wait of over two hours, another doctor appeared. He must have been called to alleviate the build-up in the waiting room, but I had no idea who he was. The nurse in the corridor then divided the files into two piles. Now my anxieties were raised again as I worried that I would be called into him instead of my consultant. Jay felt the same and reasoned this wouldn't happen. After having to wait for so long surely I would need to see the consultant that performed my surgery? The waiting went on, and on. In fact, it was nearly four hours before we were finally called in...to the registrar, not my consultant. I was devastated but what could we do? Jay was visibly annoyed as well as we entered the consulting room and the doctor introduced himself. I had to say how I was feeling.

"I thought I'd be able to see Mr Richards?"

Jay continued. "My wife has had to wait six weeks for this appointment and we've been sitting in that corridor for nearly four hours to see Mr Richards. No offence but we have no idea who you are and you don't know my wife."

The registrar did not look sympathetic, instead he took up the file from his desk.

"I have your wife's notes here so can assess her treatment myself." He fixed Jay with a cool stare then opened the paperwork and began shuffling through it.

He began reading from my notes but as he had a strong accent, we couldn't grasp what he was saying. Asking him to repeat himself met with more stony looks and heavy sighs. Attempting to find answers to our questions he leafed back and forth through my notes muttering to himself.

My tears had begun to fall, this was all wrong. The wait had been unbearable and now we were to be fobbed off with someone who knew nothing about me. As the registrar continued thumbing through the paperwork trying to familiarise himself with what I had gone through Jay and I exchanged glances and stood to leave.

"I'm sorry but we have to see Mr Richards this is not good enough." Jay took my arm and we got up to leave. The registrar did nothing to stop us as Jay led me back out to the corridor where the nurse sat at her table laden with patient files. "My wife is booked to see Mr Richards and after waiting this long, that's who we are going to see." The nurse looked from Jay to me then stood and sighed.

"I'll see what I can do."

We watched her enter the registrar's room then returning with my paperwork she knocked on Mr Richards door. It was only another ten minutes before we were finally called in to see the surgeon who had performed my operation. He stood to shake both our hands.

"Apologies for the mix up, as you can see we have been rather busy this morning."

More confident now we were finally here I spoke up, "It's not only the four hour wait today, but this appointment has also taken over six weeks to reach me and I've had no follow up in the meantime. I had to call out the local District Nurses for advice."

He sat back in his chair as he looked from me to Jay. "These appointments are generated on our system, I don't personally arrange the follow up dates and they are in line with general procedure."

"On the notes I took home from hospital it said I'd be seen within four weeks?"

"Again, I apologise, these things are out of my control." It was obvious we would need to move on, but it was still wrong. Wrong that after major surgery a patient can be left without advice or communication for so long and even then, potentially not be able to see the consultant who knows the case.

He returned to my notes. "Now, I can see here you've had another hospital admittance since your nephrectomy?" We waited while he read to himself the account of the suspected blood clot that had led to my stay in an intensive care bed. "Have you been well since that episode?"

I nodded. "Yes, well apart from back pain."

He rose and drew a sheet of blue paper across the examination bed along the wall. "I'd better have a look at the wound, if you could get onto the bed please."

Slipping out of my jacket I climbed gingerly up, the wound still hurt when I moved and my back was extremely sore. I was instructed to lift my top over the wound as the consultant began to press the area around the scarring. Once satisfied that it was healing well, I returned to my seat next to Jay.

I was then asked a series of questions about my general health and wellbeing. These weren't easy to answer as I wasn't sure if my progress post-surgery was good or bad. I still felt rough compared to what I remember before kidney cancer struck and I was experiencing a lot of pain in my back, unusually on the opposite side to the surgery. Mr Richards said this was all relative to what I had been through although he was concerned about the back pain and said quite forcibly, "This has nothing to do with my surgery."

As a precaution he booked me in for a bone scan.

Now we had a chance to ask questions and we had come prepared. This would be the first time since my admission that Jay and I could get answers together. We began with the obvious.

"Has the cancer all gone?"

He began, "The tumour was encapsulated in the kidney and both had been removed whole, therefore it should all have gone." He then explained, "While in there I had a good poke around to check surrounding organs and found no evidence of anything else sinister."

This was a huge relief and had been the question foremost in our minds. Next up, "Will there be any more treatment?"

"Kidney cancer is not generally treated with chemotherapy or radiotherapy; it doesn't respond well so therefore there will be no further treatment. You will however receive regular CT scans and blood tests."

I asked, "How long for?" The answer surprised me.

"For as long as there's a National Health Service. You are also a renal patient now so will always be on the radar. The CT scans will be six monthly for two years and continue yearly after that until five years or until we are satisfied there is no further need."

When asked if he was sure it hadn't spread, he demonstrated his answer like so. Taking a piece of paper, he made a dot with the nib of his pen.

"There could be a tumour this size inside you now, we couldn't pick it up on a scan and you wouldn't know it was there. Your choice is to leave here and worry endlessly about it or to go on living your life as best you can and hope for the best. I suggest the latter."

I was not expecting that but then, I hadn't seen cancer coming in the first place, so I suppose it makes perfect sense. Why worry about what you can't do anything about.

He went on to explain how so many elements surrounding our daily lives can cause just one cell to go wrong. What we eat, drink, even the air that we breathe holds particles that could possibly turn a single cell rogue. At least now I would be closely monitored and let's face it, I had been walking around for a long time carrying a cancerous tumour I was blissfully unaware of.

Another big question on the list was of course, 'How did it get there?' Of course, I don't want it back. I wanted to find out if my lifestyle could have had any effect or, more to the point how I could possibly avoid recurrence? I knew hardly anything about kidney cancer, information was hard to find. However, I had researched the statistics which told me it was still uncommon in women of my age. The consultant's answer was succinct.

“Walk into a children’s ward where you’ll find young people suffering with cancer and ask yourself, why them, what caused this, how come?” He went on, “If we knew the answers, we’d be better qualified to avoid this disease, sometimes there aren’t reasonable answers, sometimes it’s guesswork.”

By the time I left that day I felt that everything had been done that could have, nothing was being left to chance. Despite the wait, the consultant had answered all our questions and spent time explaining thoroughly all we needed to know. No complaints there. The next event would be the bone scan in the meantime I could worry about that small dot on the paper or, I could get on with the life I’d been given thanks to medical intervention. No contest, it was time to start living again.

PART TWO BACK TO BUSINESS

CHAPTER 28 CLIMB EVERY MOUNTAIN

Six months passed in the blink of an eye. This was remarkable considering I hadn't returned to work. The business of recovery had taken far longer than I had anticipated and this was due in part to the mental struggle of facing up to having had cancer as well as the physical restrictions it imposed on me. However, I felt the time was right to return to work and the business I'd put on the shelf.

I had phoned the tax office shortly after my diagnosis, explaining the situation and requested to close the business. Whoever I spoke to that day was not only helpful but showed a lot of empathy for my situation as he advised that I leave things as they were, keeping the business live. He said it wouldn't change anything by terminating my company and I would be as well to shelve it for a few weeks then look again at what I wanted to do. What a wise man. Six months on I was relieved to have Missfit Creations to return to. To be honest I don't know what else I would have done. Here I had a ready-made business that I could manage from home, I simply had to scale things down a little.

I worked from a spare bedroom, like small creative business up and down the country I invariably referred to it as my design studio. This housed my sewing machinery and a wardrobe full of designs as well as boxes of various haberdashery and shelves of files and books. As well as this I had a huge shed or workshop as I preferred to call it. This had industrial shelving lined with fabrics and a large rail rammed full of vintage clothing, close to one hundred items at any time.

My sewing machines were packed up, the tables folded down and most evidence of my daily work was tidied away when I returned to that room in September 2013. I had closed the website shop leaving only a homepage with a brief explanatory message saying the business was closed for the foreseeable. Looking inside the wardrobes I had a rail of stock made just before I was ill the question was did, I pick up from where I left off or make a fresh start?

The decision was stalled a little longer as we decided to have a break away to Wales. Usually our holidays would include a good deal of walking and climbing and although I wasn't 100% physically ready, we still headed for the mountains. This year we returned to one of Wales hidden treasures, a blue lagoon which was formed from an old slate mine shaft resting high in a mountain top. To get to it involved a steep climb followed by careful negotiation through a small dark tunnel cut into the rock. Alternatively, you can scramble to the top of the mountain and look down into the crystal-clear water from up high.

We had visited this beauty spot the previous year and I was determined to get to the top once more. I was nervous setting out as I found it more painful to walk up hills, each step seemed to touch whatever nerve it was that sent pain around my ribs and back. I kept going, the heat from the sun helped, as we got higher it got warmer – or rather I did. It was tough but I made it and it was well worth the effort.

Sitting beside the lagoon I was able to look back at the struggle I'd had over the previous six months with some perspective. I'd made it, got past every obstacle and climbed every mountain, literally. From my seat high in the mountains I could clearly see the progress I had made, time does heal.

On my return, the sewing machines were coming back out.

CHAPTER 29 JOINING THE GANG

Right from the start, I had found it difficult telling people about my illness. For one, it did not sit right with the fashion industry. There are more than 100 types of cancer and although kidney cancer isn't particularly well known, it has reached the top ten. Still, when I mentioned it people looked baffled. I'd heard it called the 'old man's cancer' as well which didn't do its street cred any favours.

The other reason was the attention the C word drew. I understood the shock when people discovered I'd had cancer, even the sympathy but it also attracted anecdotes. You know the sort of thing.

'My Dad had lung cancer.' Cue extended story.

'My neighbour's having chemo.' Wait while full details given.

'I felt a lump in my breast.' Hear all about their anxieties.

Don't get me wrong, I understood this was par for the course. Cancer is a huge conversation piece. Everyone knows someone who's suffered. Whether a family member, friend, neighbour or of course a celebrity. However, when I was regaled with stories about Kylie Minogue's struggle or Auntie Connie's wig dilemma, I switched off. It was as though my cancer diagnosis made me an aficionado on the subject. I felt I'd been redefined from fashion to cancer victim. My specialist subject on Mastermind was no longer pop fashion of the 80s, I was now expert in the causes and treatment of cancer. Except I wasn't and I didn't want to talk about it. Therefore, when an explanation was needed as to the abandonment of my business I was constantly put on the spot.

I thought the Facebook post I'd written a few weeks after diagnosis would take most of that burden away but then, not everyone has Facebook. Also, it was time I started getting out again and meeting people, I couldn't conduct my life from a laptop forever.

Once I'd made the decision to return to work, I needed to redefine the direction of my business. I couldn't shake the idea that my work was somehow responsible for my illness. I still felt there was something superficial and unworthy about some of the shows and catwalk exhibitions I'd partaken in despite the main focus of my company being on sustainable fashion. I began clearing out my workshop, filling large bags with fabrics I decided I would never use again. By the time I'd finished there were twelve full bin bags of materials and haberdashery. I then divided this up, most I would donate to local colleges for fashion students. Some I'd keep back and the rest I'd take to the local Cancer Centre. I'd donated items to this small local charity in the past as they ran an arts and crafts session once a week. I figured I could go along with my stash and, now I had more time to myself I could maybe help. It would get me out of the house and I'd be meeting people.

Sharon Fox had set up the Cancer Centre after her own battle with breast cancer. They now had premises in the town and a large following of dedicated volunteers as well as the cancer patients and their families who benefited from the services provided. Sharon was aware of my illness. She'd left a lovely message in response to my Facebook announcement, so I contacted her to say I'd be going along to the craft meeting that week.

When I arrived at the centre, I was overcome with all kinds of emotions, fear, anxiety, sadness, panic. Pulling up in the car park it had suddenly dawned on me; once I step through that door they'll know. I wasn't only dropping off a donation, I was now one of their gang! It was as though the news hit me all over again. The people behind that door could see right through the bravado because they'd been there too.

Whilst I stood outside, another lady arrived and as if via telepathy, greeted me and opened the door, ushering me in like were old friends. Once inside, Sharon saw me and I was effortlessly introduced to everyone present (no mention of the C word) saying that I was joining the craft group that morning.

After making idle chatter for a few minutes we walked through to another room where I was told one of the crafters, Maggie would show me what they had been working on. So far, so good. It was warm and relaxed and I was talking about things I could relate to.

Then it hit me again. I can't describe what or why. It was as though I was looking at the activity and hearing the chatter from a distance. Tears started to fall (incidentally they are falling again now even thinking about it) and I stood and cried. For the first time, outside of my home or a hospital bed the emotion was overwhelming, and I let go of some of the fear I'd been hiding.

Maggie comforted me and said all the right things before another couple of ladies offered me a seat in the office to chat about how I could help. In fact, they were helping me. By this time, I was able to articulate how I was feeling but they already knew. By the time I left that morning I felt strangely empowered. For the first time I had cried in public about my experience and talked openly about cancer and it was ok. I was ok. It had taken my kidney and knocked my health about somewhat, but I was still here.

After that initial visit I returned to the centre a few times, admittedly not as many as I'd planned and I made no firm commitments. Admittedly, one of those visits was spent in the car park and I didn't leave my car...bad day. However, when I did venture in, I wasn't the new girl. I witnessed many other men and women enter the centre and speak about their illness; this was a most humbling experience. There was no judgement nor patronising, no one compared scars whether mental or physical. This was a safe place, one where I knew I could retreat if I needed reassurance or join in when I wanted to prove that cancer hadn't taken the best of me.

CHAPTER 30 THE KETOGENIC DIET

I had never been on a diet. Between the age of 18 and 45, apart from pregnancy, I had never gone over 9 stone / 126 pounds. I am a little over 5'7" and had always been happy with my weight. This isn't to say that my appearance hasn't caused me upset over the years. I was bullied at school for being a skinny child, given the nick name 'dog bone' does nothing for your self-confidence. Never having put on significant weight meant I was fair game for all the clichés; you'll blow away one day, you'd have to run around in the rain to get wet, there's nothing of you, etc. It hurts, I know I speak for countless slim people when I say this. The downside of not carrying excessive weight is being without curves, another cause for a multitude of teasing and ridicule as I grew up. In fact, it never ceases as more recently we've been subjected to the popular phrase, 'Real Women Have Curves'. Does that mean the rest of us are fake? I have been incensed by the bullying of models condemned for their lack of humps and bumps which presumably they've starved themselves to lose. OK, some models will strive to conform to the standard catwalk physique however, many are born that way, it's not a choice. To be ridiculed and called out for being too thin is easily as harmful to a person's confidence as telling them they're too fat. Some of us don't have a choice.

I recognised that the same rule should apply to overweight people as I met cancer patients who were taking a cocktail of drugs, often steroid based. At the cancer centre I met women who, prior to cancer had fitted size 8/10 clothes and whose wardrobe had increased to size 18/20. They'd been subjected to gruelling treatments where they lost all their hair and then gained several pounds in weight, naturally confidence dropping away in abundance.

Becoming a cancer patient myself had taught me to be less judgemental, you really don't know what the person standing next to you is going through. There may be good reason why they look sad or their clothes don't fit properly. It's frequently said that we're none of us happy with our size or weight, well some of us may be and others don't have a choice. Perhaps the phrase should be 'Other people are never happy with our size?'

Before going into hospital, I was probably the healthiest weight I'd ever been, hovering around 9 stone. It's ironic really as I was also carrying a large tumour in my kidney. I've always been active; up and out early with the dog, running around for work as well as a busy home life and Jay and I walked most evenings, it's a good way to catch up on the day and beats sitting in front of the TV. Apart from that though I did no structured exercise, I'd never visited a gym, taken classes like Zumba or yoga and certainly not monitored my food intake. That's not to say I didn't eat a healthy diet. I was vegetarian for around 10 years until I was tempted by a bacon sandwich...apparently the downfall of many veggies. Although I began eating meat again, it was minimal and I always had far more fruit and veg than my five a day.

Post cancer, I was searching for answers, looking for blame. Something triggered these cells to go rogue, was it meat, alcohol, air pollution? There had to be a reason and so I began a process of elimination. Alcohol was a no brainer.

There was no denying it, I had drunk too much. Weeknights we would go for our usual walk and talk then on the way home I would often call into the corner shop for a bottle of wine. They sometimes had a brand on offer, three for £10 so it made sense to take them up on it. Therefore, on reflection I would generally drink around three bottles every week. Weekends were another matter. We'd often take the short walk into town where there were a variety of pubs and bars. I only drank lager when out, mostly bottles like Corona. My average input would be six bottles, but this could just as easily be six pints on a big night out. When visiting friends for a catch up the level of alcohol could increase further and if there was a party, well, who counts?

Meat often followed drink. It was after (or maybe during) a session at friends when I 'allegedly' ate a bacon sandwich whilst still a veggie. Whatever, it was closely followed by gammon, egg and chips at a pub lunch! The other post drink favourite was to go to the 'dirty burger' van, you can't beat a big, meaty beef burger with onions and red sauce the morning after the night before.

These confessions are not to say I was a binge drinking, fad eater. In fact, when questioned by a doctor prior to surgery I struggled to give an accurate drink estimate, telling him I may have a glass of wine of an evening. I thought my drinking was extremely moderate. For one reason, I didn't get drunk. I never mixed drinks, took shots or spirits. I wasn't loud or lairy, I'm very non-confrontational and didn't make a song and dance about drinking (unless you count the occasional Irish jig after one too many). Jay was on hand to correct me, giving the doctor a more truthful account of my midweek wine consumption, it wasn't excessive, but it was definitely too much.

Kidney cancer made me sit up and take more notice of what I ate and drank. Despite no clear link between my diet and the tumour, there were positive changes to be made and I intended to make them.

For starters I took note of the suggestions for healthy eating given on the kidney cancer charity page. Most of the advice centred on a varied, well balanced diet and practicing moderation with foods high in sugars or fats.

One of the newly diagnosed kidney cancer patients I hooked up with was Lisanne Vos who had also set up a blog journaling about her experience. Lisanne had focussed on health tips, exercise and recipes for a healthy life which gave me another source of inspiration for the physical changes I felt I needed to make.

The book that I really took to heart was lent to me by Sharon Fox at the Cancer Centre, The Cantin Ketogenic Diet - for Cancer, Type1 Diabetes & other ailments. The author modified the tried and tested ketogenic diet to allegedly overcome the aggressive breast cancer diagnosis she'd been given. She also claims that her son's Type 1 diabetes was no match for her modified ketogenic diet as he was able to live life without the aid of insulin.

The diet itself cut out both dairy and sugar. As I was mostly vegetarian, rarely eating meat or fish this meant I was veering towards being vegan. I swapped milk for soya and bought dairy free spreads and cheese alternatives, which incidentally tasted like sawdust. Not being one for chocolate or cake, I wasn't hit hard by the lack of sweeties, but no dairy began taking its toll quickly. My energy levels dropped dramatically and despite feeling lethargic I wasn't sleeping well either. Regardless of this, I continued with the diet believing it was a case of my body adjusting to its new food regime, things would improve and soon I'd be feeling better that I ever had and stray cancer cells would be obliterated.

CHAPTER 31 BONE SCAN

The appointment for the bone scan, recommended by the consultant arrived a couple of weeks after I saw him. Ruby drove me to the hospital that morning and we were directed to the reassuringly named Nuclear Medicine Department. Once a canular was inserted into my wrist, a specialist nurse explained how she would then pump some 'stuff' into me.

"It's the best way to describe it." She continued. "The stuff will flow around your body enabling the scanner to pick up what it needs from your bones." Suitably worried I didn't question further, having already learnt not to Google medical queries I decided against quizzing the nurse about the stuff flowing through my veins.

Once this was fully administered, I could leave the hospital for 90 minutes. During this time, I was told to drink plenty and most importantly, "Keep away from small children, babies and pregnant mothers." Apparently, this was due to the slight risk of radiation I was carrying. It seemed the 'stuff' contained gamma rays! For the next few hours, I would be superhuman.

Not enticed by the hospital canteen we headed for the nearest Wetherspoons which, of a weekday lunchtime had a surprising number of young Mums and kids. Tucking ourselves away in a corner we ordered a light bite and I looked menacingly at any toddlers that approached our table.

Back at the hospital, I was taken into the scan room and asked to climb onto the bed fully clothed. The specialist nurse explained how the scanner would come down so close that it would almost touch my face and that I shouldn't feel alarmed. Making sure I was positioned correctly; she then left the room. The following 20 minutes was spent lying perfectly still while this huge machine lowered itself down to within a whisker of my nose and slowly moved across my body. I wouldn't say I was claustrophobic, but it was a freaky feeling, I did worry it was a bone crusher!

When the scanner had taken all the images it needed, the specialist returned to the room. Before I could leave, she gave this important instruction.

"For the next 48 hours steer clear of Mums to be and children and each time you have a wee, flush the chain twice as a small amount of radiation may be left behind."

That night I had the sensation of glowing in the dark, like a carcinogenic super-hero.

The results of the scan took a long time to appear. I went through the familiar routine; jumping when the letterbox sounded, touching the phone to make sure it was on the hook. It was six weeks before a letter did drop onto the mat, this was over three months post-surgery. Within the envelope's window, immediately below the address was scrawled in biro, 'Bone scan normal'. The postman knew before I did!

When I opened it, the letter contained the information I should have been given when leaving hospital after surgery. Detailing the size and grade of the tumour along with personal details, it was way overdue. Whilst I was happy with the work of the consultant and his team in ridding me of the cancerous tumour, where admin is concerned, the words 'must try harder' spring to mind. Despite the crass delivery of the result, it was excellent news. Another worry to cross off the list.

The trouble with having had a cancer diagnosis is that when you become unwell, your thoughts are unavoidably drawn to more sinister reasons for illness. Pre-cancer, there was a rational voice in my head telling me I most likely had a virus and I'd feel better soon.

My back pain had increased and I felt sick, lacking energy. I was also feverish. I felt so poorly I had to stay in bed which seemed a massive backward step after several months' recovery. In bed, unwell now had bad connotations. I'd rarely been unable to drag myself out because of illness before. In the same way, problems were magnified at night, I felt even worse staying in bed. Unable to do anything, my mind worked overtime. What if it's back?

A visit to my GP was inconclusive, symptoms pointed to a virus. Also, with a CT scan due in a couple of weeks it was best to wait for the outcome. He was however extremely understanding, seeing how awful I was feeling he asked me to return a week later. He was also interested to learn I had taken on the ketogenic diet and made no qualms about dismissing this 'fad eating plan.'

"It's making you ill," he said. "There's no firm evidence to suggest dairy will harm your kidney, take everything in moderation." I had to admit mealtime wasn't as good in the absence of cheese, eggs and milk and I'd lost nearly half a stone since taking it on.

When I went back a week later, I was feeling relatively good again having shaken off the 'sorry for myself' feeling and putting the negative thoughts to bed. I'd also reintroduced some dairy back into mealtimes. I don't think my dietary changes were the sole cause of my illness, but my health certainly didn't improve by ditching the dairy. Moderation would have to be my new mantra.

CHAPTER 32 THE MORNING AFTER THE NIGHT BEFORE

The problem I had with making new business plans was the fear I now harboured of everything crashing down around me once again. The 'what ifs'. I also continued to view the fashion business with disdain, it seemed so superficial. What lies beneath the fabrics, latest trends, must have designs for the season? Does it mean anything?

I'd frequently been disparaging about the fashion industry in the past, especially the language used, rocking a look, working a trend. As for the social media traps being pushed; Like my Page or Follow Back, they still made me cringe. It hadn't stopped me being part of it though, principles don't bring in customers and cash. I was as guilty as the next fashionista for clocking up the comments, likes and followers.

The passion was missing now though. Like me or not, heart my designs or don't, nothing mattered unless it felt genuine.

One incident that really brought this home to me involved an acquaintance in the fashion world with whom I'd never exactly hit it off. Tensions between associates working in the same field isn't uncommon but this was unfounded. She just gave me a wide berth generally and seemed particularly false whenever we met. However, after my cancer diagnosis she became extremely friendly, it appeared heartfelt and I was quite touched, until I heard she was going to name a design after me. This again wasn't uncommon with independent designers, giving a dress or accessory someone's name for whatever reason. But I wouldn't wear any of this designer's gear and the spin on it appeared to relate to my cancer. Thankfully, a Debbie design was never created and her attentions vanished as quickly as they'd appeared. It had reminded me of what a superficial world I worked in though, did I really want that again? I hadn't hesitated to close the business after diagnosis, six months later I was inventing excuses to delay its return. I was on the outside looking in and had a clearer picture it seemed. I felt like a hypocrite criticising people in that circle when I'd walked the same walk, talked the same talk. The fight for online superiority and sales is more like a popularity contest.

Was that the voice of experience or was it the experience of cancer speaking to me? Stripped of my fashionista image, lying in a hospital bed, attached to numerous machines, I thought little about the cancer inside me. Seven months on with recovery going well I thought about it often. Let's face it, I'd been carrying that tumour around with me a fair few years according to medical science. Me and my cancer had done Clothes Shows together, arranged many fashion events and strutted about town in our glad rags for a while. Perhaps that was it, I couldn't separate the cancer from the business. I had to allocate blame. After diagnosis I was told to give the tumour a name.

"Choose a person you dislike," they said.

I couldn't bear to think of a person I detest invading my kidney and causing so much pain, so I ignored that advice. Now I feel that it was made up of all the things I worked for that were never meant to be. Is this common in cancer survivors? Is the fashion industry so disdainful or is my reaction a natural response to the shock of having cancer? Had I worked in any other sector would I have the same disrespect for my career? All I did know was that the scars were taking longer to heal than I expected and they ran far deeper than I knew.

Maybe it was those inner demons, questioning my motives for returning to work in the fashion industry that led to some serious rule breaking. The unwritten rules that I self-imposed post-surgery and after the realisation that life as I know it would have to change. These included giving up salt and alcohol.

My misdemeanour involved eating a bag of salt and vinegar crisps and drinking three glasses of red wine. Putting this into perspective with my prior vino consumption, not to mention the amount of salt I shook on most meals, it's not the worst thing I could have done. However, the morning after I felt bad. Not hungover, as although I'd resisted wine for several months, I don't think my alcohol tolerance had declined much. I simply felt a failure with no willpower.

The reason I gave in to the demon drink and crisps was that the following morning I was going for my six-month CT scan – which was eight months post-surgery. Deny as I might, I was a little worried about my trip back through all seeing tunnel.

Waking up I felt guilty for indulging in those things that were on the banned list. But then, given what I used to drink I daresay 'a little bit of what you fancy really can do you good.' I suppose moderation is the key. This minor lapse was more about Dutch Courage and the need to relax, forget for a night why I had such Do's and Don'ts. Hopefully when my results came in, I could raise a glass in celebration.

My appointment was late afternoon at the District Hospital. Joey drove me over and we arrived in plenty of time which was good as the barrier to the main car park wasn't working so queues were building up. Thanks to some nifty driving, Joey managed to negotiate a way through the waiting cars to another car park on the other side of the hospital.

A brisk walk through the maze of buildings brought us to the X-Ray Department where I checked in and was directed along another corridor to the CT scanning room. We seated ourselves with others already waiting, some in gowns with jugs of water. I'd been instructed previously to drink plenty as the contrast wouldn't agree with my lone kidney. Another couple of people came after me, still no one at the desk and in the meantime, there was a line of emergency patients on stretchers and in wheelchairs. No one spoke.

When finally a nurse appeared, he looked around the room, sighed deeply and took the name of the person sitting nearest who had arrived last. The lady next to me ventured, "Excuse me, I've been waiting longer, my appointment was meant to be an hour ago."

"Well I wasn't here then," replied the nurse, barely looking at her.

It's a wonder he hadn't noticed her as she wore a fluffy leopard print dressing gown and glittery slippers. Other patients began grumbling to each other about the length of time they'd been sitting and lack of organisation. Sarcastic nurse was in danger of hyperventilating if he didn't stop sighing as deeply.

When I was eventually booked in, I asked about a jug of water. After a quick glance at his notes the nurse replied, "You don't need one."

I presumed no contrast dye would be fed through (usually the reason to drink plenty of water beforehand) and left it at that.

Another nurse came around and I was given a carrier bag and two hospital gowns with the instruction to put both on: one opening to the front, the other to the back. I'd worn a fair few of these gowns over the past few months and remained puzzled as to why the design was so impractical and dated. They all had a similar geometric pattern in a range of washed-out colours and the same fiddly ties at the neck. The lack of dignity they provide is notorious which is why we are so often instructed to wear two at a time. I suppose one thing that can be said is that the hospital gown is a great leveller, anyone wearing one immediately loses their individuality as well as their pride. Together with me in this waiting room there could be lawyers and cleaners, fashionistas and frumps, it'd be difficult to tell the difference, although some of the footwear gave the game away. One chap sitting opposite had a pair of builder's rigger boots showing below the hem of his gown, definite lawyer!

Sarcastic nurse had at least broken the ice and a hum of chatter now filled the waiting room. The glamorous lady next to me told me she was there for her three-year check-up as a kidney cancer patient. She then went on to say her husband had fought kidney cancer but lost his battle just before her own diagnosis. *What are the chances?* She was terrified of bad news. I listened on as she explained how she'd been suffering from fatigue and blood in her urine but put it down to the stress of looking after her terminally ill husband. She had visited her GP several times during this period, but no tests were offered. After her husband's untimely death, she decided to pursue the matter, returning to her GP and demanding to see a specialist. By the time she was referred, her tumour was the size of a tennis ball and the prognosis not good. I was discovering that no matter how painful my own experience had been, there really is someone else worse off.

It wasn't long before I was called through to an annex room where a canular was put into the back of my hand to feed the contrast dye through. I asked should I have been given a jug of water to drink and told once again it wasn't necessary? This seemed odd as it was something I'd been told to expect and other patients appeared to have had one.

There were a few jugs of water on tables in the waiting room that appeared to have been used. As I resolved to ask again my name was called and I was taken through to the scanning room.

"Have you drunk the full litre of water?" The nurse inside asked.

"I was told I didn't need to?" I said.

She shook her head and told me she'd have a word with someone, a bit too late for me though as I was being positioned on the scanning bed.

"Can I suck a throat lozenge?" I asked. I'd had an irritating cough and although much better, I was bound to cough when the machine started up.

"As long as you don't choke," was the reply.

Being my third CT scan, I was aware of the procedure; the breath holding, moving through the donut and the weird sensation of the contrast dye pumping through with that delightful sensation of wetting yourself. Afterwards I asked about results as no appointment had been sent through to see my consultant yet. I was told as it was the consultant who had requested the scan, I'd have to be patient.

Watch and wait.

CHAPTER 33 PATIENCE PATIENT

I'd had an extra two months to wait for my six-month scan and now I'd have to bide my time until the results came through. Once again, I began listening for the letterbox, checking the phone was on the hook, carrying my mobile into every room. Scanxiety was a new one though as having such a rapid introduction to cancer and surgery I'd not had to wait for scan results. I was losing sleep, it was no good, I'd have to make a call myself.

Three weeks after my hospital visit, I phoned the consultant's secretary who sounded mildly irritated on answering saying, "Can you hold I'm in the middle of something important."

On her return to the phone she explained how long scan results can take to come through, saying three weeks was not lengthy by any means. I said I understood but the scan had been two months late and I worried the results may take equally as long. After an audible sigh she asked the usual questions.

"Name, date of birth, hospital number?"

After feeding her all the information needed, I didn't expect the response.

"No, we don't appear to have you on record."

"What? Mr Richards took my kidney out, I'd kind of hoped you'd have something?"

"Bear with me."

A lengthy pause before she came back.

"Yes fine."

"Fine you've found me?" I ventured.

"Your scan's fine." Came back.

"My scan's normal, no more cancer?"

"Yes fine, ok?" The tone of voice said, can I go now.

"Ok, thanks." *I think?*

Whether it was the waver in my voice or that she simply caught herself on, the secretary's tone changed.

"You must feel quite abandoned?"

"You could say that it's not been the greatest experience, trying to get information." I wanted to be angry, to let all the frustration pour out but she sounded genuine.

"I'm sorry." There was nothing more she could add. My case was unfortunately typical, not a one-off matter that had slipped under the radar. What else could she say?

And that was it. First lot of results back and its good news, delivered in the worst way.

I wanted to feel happy and elated but the way the news was relayed made me annoyed and frustrated. The relief came sometime after.

I wasn't due to see the consultant until the twelve-month anniversary of my surgery. Going on delays so far this would no doubt stretch to eighteen months. There were so many things I needed to ask the consultant when I finally got to see him again. Questions about my treatment, diagnosis and surgery. Also questions about the care, or lack of it that was given during this time. I decided the best way to do so would be in a letter. I needed him to feel what I felt if that were possible. So far, he'd not displayed any empathy.

I wrote about my treatment so far. The lack of aftercare, missing notes, follow up appointments and scan that exceeded the times given. I questioned the presence of a 'dirty big tumour' as I hadn't received dedicated cancer care. I'd never met a specialist nurse, not been handed a single fact sheet or advised of any support.

I detailed the only letter I'd received in June containing the few lines of histology, a note I apparently should have travelled home with in March. The same note of which had my bone scan result scrawled in the window envelope.

Apart from the actual surgery, what exactly had he done? Had Jay not intervened when we attended the post op appointment, I'd have ended up seeing a registrar I'd never set eyes on before and who knew nothing of my surgery. It was inexcusable.

I relayed some of the answers he gave to our questions which, looking back were mildly amusing, almost philosophical.

Q. "How long have I had the tumour?"

A. "How far can a horse run?"

I'd thought it reasonable to ask about prevention, lifestyle, diet, anything I should or shouldn't do to stop it returning. My Aunt died of kidney cancer; my father had kidney problems. How do I put an experience like this behind me without asking questions?

I told him about the notes taken from my hospital journal that had become a blog. How I'd had to leave some parts out though as rather than give hope, my experience could bewilder and frighten patients facing kidney cancer surgery.

My GP got a mention as he'd had to pick up the care that the hospital failed to give. Most importantly, he had listened to me and not once dismissed my fears. He answered questions where he could and gave help and advice when needed.

In case the consultant needed reminding of who I was I inserted links of where he could read my blog, advising he start at the beginning as he missed my arrival and the haphazard diagnosis. As I rounded my letter off, I bore my soul, telling him how I wanted nothing more than to put this experience behind me and be free of cancer and its current hold on my attention. It was then that the words I'd not yet spoken fell on to the page.

I don't think I can trust your ability to continue as my consultant if I feel you don't care.

I've been left feeling my kidney cancer was insignificant. I don't want to feel this way anymore and so will be seeking alternative care.

The letter was never sent.

CHAPTER 34 THE CHEMO QUESTION

A question I got frequently asked was, 'Did you have chemotherapy?' The answer is no. Apparently chemo doesn't generally work as kidney cancer is resistant to it. The most common course of action with kidney cancer is surgery and if needed, targeted therapies like immunotherapy.

Thankfully, surgery did the trick for me. Saying that, there is an element of watch and wait involved which is why regular scans are put in place. Despite adopting a positive mindset and attempting to push all thoughts of it returning away, it never truly leaves.

My Mom's breast cancer tumour was several centimetres smaller than my lump and was graded the same. She received both chemotherapy and radiotherapy as well as taking chemo drugs for a further seven years following surgery. I attended her final appointment with the oncologist where, I expected she would leave feeling elated, treatment finally over. On the contrary, she was bereft, it was as though a crutch had been kicked from under her, no more drugs, no further follow up. Even though it was a gruelling few weeks of chemo that brought with it horrendous side effects, my Mom, like many cancer patients seemed to relish the thought that their cancer was being zapped, kicked out, obliterated. I had none of that. No sooner had I learnt it was in me, it was evicted. Whether it had spread its cells elsewhere, only time would tell. No-one wishes they could have chemo but faced with no targeted drug treatment whatsoever it felt like leaving things to chance.

I guess my lack of obvious treatment was the reason I was able to get on with life without much disruption. For a good while it was painful to walk far, even sitting for too long hurt. However, my appearance didn't scream 'cancer victim.' I could just as well have pulled a muscle in my leg or be nursing a hangover. Visibly I was clearly slower, more awkward and a little cautious.

One of my first solo trips out was to the local chip shop. Georges is only a short walk up the road so I insisted I'd be ok to go alone, I'd missed getting up and getting on with things and this was a start. So, that Friday chippy tea night I walked carefully up and took my place in the queue. One of the reason's it's the best chippy in town is the staff, the banter is priceless. No sooner was I in the door than one of the regular staff, Deb greeted me.

"Alright Deb, where've you been, ain't seen you in ages?"

The shop was busy and a line of heads turned their attention to our conversation.

"I've erm, not been well." I ventured. *Please don't ask what with.*

"What's wrong then, you've been gone a while?" Deb continued shovelling chips from the fryer while she waited for my reply. There was no escape.

In a low whisper over the counter. "I've had cancer."

"OH MY GOD! What kind?" Deb stood motionless, one hand on her hip the other balancing a battered cod on a spatula.

"Kidney." I murmured.

"Bloody hell, Deb, did they take it out?"

By this stage anyone contemplating a steak and kidney pie was reviewing their options. The conversation continued in this way, a medical Q&A over a counter of fried food until it was my turn to be served. After taking my order the young girl serving me mouthed,

"It looks good." Smiling she nodded at my hair. It took a moment and then...

"Oh no!" I laughed. "It's not a wig, I haven't had chemo."

This was the first of a few similarly amusing encounters I've had when the subject of my having had cancer arises. It's generally presumed that cancer and chemo go hand in hand.

A few years previously, when I accompanied my Mom to her chemotherapy after breast cancer, I had a similar experience. I took her to every appointment and at the time my hair was in multicoloured dreadlocks. Other patients would regularly presume that I was the patient because my hair must be false. What I hadn't anticipated was that my real hair would raise the same speculation!

CHAPTER 35 DESIGNED FOR CANCER

As 2014 began, I needed the New Year to mean something, more than resolutions. My word for 2014 was Positivity. With the help of my GP I had managed to change hospital trusts and my treatment would now be with the District Hospital. A short while before Christmas, Ruby came with me to meet the consultant taking on my care, Miss Khan and she was the polar opposite of the previous one.

Unfortunately, none of my notes had been transferred from Central and so she didn't have any history of my case so this was only a meet and greet. As introductions go it was good, I even got a hug off her. She explained that a meeting would take place with other specialists at the hospital in January where they would discuss my case. From there we would meet again; the only warning signal was when referring to the letter received from my previous consultant. She spoke of him by first name and voiced surprise at why I'd want to leave his care.

My back pain had continued and had moved up and underneath my ribs. Sitting for long periods was more uncomfortable so I needed to move frequently to relieve the pain. My GP prescribed a drug called Gabapentin to combat this. I've never been a fan of pain meds, now especially as I only have one kidney. However, paracetomol just wasn't cutting it and to function fully I needed help.

One thing's for sure, I didn't have the pain prior to surgery and I'm eager to know what my new consultant makes of it.

My GP continued to be very proactive in my care recommending McKenzie back exercises and suggested yoga or Pilates may help. I found a local Pilates class and went along with my friend Fi. Neither of us had ever been to an exercise class before and had no idea of the protocol. Neither did we have the gear! Fi also works in the creative industry, amongst her many talents she used to put my hair in dreadlocks and still had a multicoloured head of dreads herself. We both preferred alternative fashion and so our wardrobes didn't include sportswear. I had continued to invest in more comfortable clothing and so had a pair of Adidas jogging bottoms and cartoon tee shirt. Fi dug out some bright leggings and a band tee shirt. When we walked into the Pilates studio and faced a room of people in mostly black leggings and neutral tops, we felt a little out of place.

The guy taking the class was extremely enthusiastic and welcomed us loudly, attracting more attention. I attempted to take him to one side and mention why I was there as naturally I didn't expect to be able to join in the majority of the class. Discretion wasn't in his nature though and the rest of the class were witness to his 'Oh my Gods' and 'Oh bless yous' as I explained my limitations. Once the session got started Fi and I were both soon out of our depth and our giggles got out of control. I found myself sitting back watching a lot of the exercises as they involved using core strength, of which I had little. Even after almost a year it felt as though my abdomen could tear open at any time. The end of class couldn't come too soon and we made a hasty exit. Pilates was now crossed off my to do list and I wasn't in a hurry to attempt yoga.

I was still struggling to see how cancer and fashion could work together. However, there's a hell of a lot of us affected by this disease one way or another. Not only does it affect your health, it can play havoc with your wardrobe.

I'm not being flippant here. You ask someone who's had the trauma of mastectomy about bra shopping or a person who's undergone abdominal surgery about waistbands. This is without even going down the chemo route and how hair loss affects your confidence. From the hospital bed to the supermarket aisle, no matter where we are – how you look will undoubtedly affect how you feel.

My relationship with the humble hospital gown had been too close for comfort over the past few months. So it was that I decided to make it my new project, there had to be a better way. Not only the gown, I wanted to design a range of clothing and accessories for cancer patients and those with long term illness with a fashion conscience. Just because you receive a damning diagnosis doesn't mean you have to abandon your dress sense and forget about your individuality. There were already many wonderful products on the market designed specifically with cancer patients in mind, the difference I wanted to add was individuality. It was the first time in over twelve months that I was excited about a project. I wanted to get back to work. I had purpose again and my head was buzzing with ideas, chemo headscarves, bags to disguise drips and drains, mastectomy tops and customised hospital gowns. The designs kept coming. Finally, work that would make a difference. Through my association with the local cancer centre I was even planning workshops where people could come to relax and create something of benefit to themselves or a patient they knew.

After all the doubts I'd had concerning getting back to business, the answer had been staring me in the face. Fashion didn't have to be superficial. Elasticated waists aren't only for kids and the elderly. Hospital gowns shouldn't have to be as bland and undignified. The trick was to make them look good, add some personality, now that was something I knew a lot about. Cancer does not have to dictate how we look and feel about our appearance.

My revolutionary new hospital gown design idea came when I was sorting through some vintage stock. Amongst the 1960s dresses I found a wrap over that was intended as a beach dress. From that I drew out a pattern for a gown, the body of which could be made in one piece without seams. It could be worn with or without sleeves and would be put on as you would a coat, the difference being there was an extra armhole that wrapped over the first. This meant a gown that eliminated fastenings and covered your dignity, no gaps. Easy to access and simple to make.

It seemed too good to be true, so I set to work searching the net, looking for something similar but nothing. I trawled though hospital gown providers and worded my searches every which way and still it seemed I was on to something that hadn't been done before. A definite eureka moment!

I was wearing another hospital gown before too long as I was sent by my GP for an ultrasound scan. I had begun experiencing some unexplained bleeding and he advised I get this checked out. Without going into too much detail, this involved something that resembled the long, slim microphone the presenter, Terry Wogan used in the TV quiz show Blankety Blank! I will not be filling in any blanks as to where this was put, let's just say it was *blanking* undignified!

The results were sent to my GP who told me there was nothing sinister lurking in that area so all good. The back pain continued and so the Gabapentin dose was increased. I was already wary of taking this drug and voiced my concerns as they seem so hard hitting. The doctor said there was nothing to worry about, there would be no side effects harmful to my solo kidney, so I agreed to up the dose.

The reason for ongoing pain in my abdomen was looking more likely to be due to nerve damage. Despite the protestations of my surgeon who insisted my discomfort had nothing to do with his surgery, I didn't hurt like this before. The back pain could be a knock-on effect of poor posture because of my abdominal pain. The event that replayed in my mind was of when the hospital physiotherapist had made me stand and walk, resulting in my collapse only a day after surgery. That wasn't physio it was torture, and while it may not have contributed to ongoing issues, they maybe could have been avoided had she actually looked at my condition and suggested exercises that could help.

**The McKenzie method was developed in the 1950s by physical therapist, Robin McKenzie in New Zealand. He developed a series of manoeuvres and exercises to help patients take a more active role in their continued health. The exercises are used to extend the spine, helping to centralize the patient's pain. The long-term goal is to teach patients how to treat themselves, managing pain using exercise.*

CHAPTER 36 WRONG FOOTED

Finally, after weeks of waiting I received the confirmation in writing from my new consultant which read:

'We have now managed to get hold of your scan from Central. This does not show any evidence of spread or abnormalities.'

At last I had the reassurance and peace of mind I'd waited over three months for, just a shame I'd had to move hospital to get it. Despite having heard from the consultant's secretary that everything was 'fine,' there had been no written confirmation nor had my GP received anything. The letter also invited me to discuss how to proceed with my care at an appointment where I would meet the consultant again. This time though, she would be in possession of the facts – as would I which meant we could take up from where Central Hospital left off.

I was still angry and upset looking back on what could have been a far more straightforward and painless experience. It certainly appeared to have been a lack of communication that led to most of the poor care I received from the Central team. However, there is no doubt that the disease itself, kidney cancer has been neglected as far as care packages go. From the moment I was admitted the uncertainty and neglect were often down to lack of information rather than lack of actual care. Even my diagnosis was a farce.

I was prepared with a list of questions again. As this list had been put together several months post-surgery, it included questions about why certain things didn't happen or indeed weren't investigated. I was hoping to discover conclusively why I now suffered ongoing back and abdominal pain and how to alleviate it. I was also hoping to learn more about diet and exercise which had been overlooked by my previous consultant.

The nerves I'd experienced when approaching appointments at Central were replaced by hopeful anticipation as I set off to see Miss Khan. I decided to walk the three miles to the local hospital where the meeting was scheduled to take place, or so I thought. It was a fine day, but we'd had a significant amount of rainfall and the shortcut I took across a meadow had not been a good idea. The path had looked ok at the start but by the time I reached the middle of the field I began sinking. My black trainers were dirty brown by the time I reached the other side. Arriving at the local hospital I headed straight for the toilets where I attempted to scrape as much mud as possible off my trainers with paper towels before presenting myself breathlessly to reception. I looked as though I'd just completed a cross country race. The administrator looked from the letter I'd handed over, to her screen then back at me.

"It's not here I'm afraid, you're meant to be at the District Hospital."

She passed the letter back, pointing out the now obvious location of my appointment. I remained speechless due to the lump in my throat.

"Don't worry, I'll phone and let them know you're here and ask them to rearrange, you'll get another appointment through soon I'm sure."

I nodded my thanks and turned for the exit holding back tears. Miss Khan would think me a complete idiot now, unable to read a letter properly. The hospital I'd arrived at was part of the same Trust and was mentioned in the letter heading which, I'd presumed was the venue where my appointment would take place. Wrong.

I'd built today's appointment up so large in my head that I felt crushed now and the three mile walk home seemed more like ten. En route I stopped off at Sainsbury's for some shopping, I may as well have something to show for my epic ordeal. Against my better judgement I used the self-checkout which succeeded in making me look more ridiculous than I already felt with its chorus of 'unexpected item in baggage area' on repeat. My tears were falling as I left the store, what a disaster of a day.

A couple of weeks later I made it. Right date, time and hospital. Finally, I would be able to discuss my latest scan result and get an expert opinion on how my care would proceed. Our meeting began warm and friendly again with the consultant allowing me to view the scan images myself, the first time I'd come face to face with my cancerous invader.

She explained that my case had been discussed by an MDT (multidisciplinary team made up of healthcare professionals from different disciplines) where it was agreed that my cancer had been fully excised. She then went on to explain that my tumour had been Grade 2, a low grade, which was also good news as there's less chance of it returning. The next fact she presented that really puzzled me was the size of the tumour which she described as 5cm. I queried this as it had been measured as 7cm throughout my stay in hospital. Flicking through her notes she arrived at a sheet of paper with an account of the post-operative biopsy which gave the tumour dimension as 5cm. Puzzling? It would be some time before I discovered Miss Khan hadn't read my notes thoroughly enough to realise the tumour had been shrunk during embolisation and was in fact 7cm. What she said next took me even more by surprise.

"Taking all this information into account and the fact that you're relatively young and leading a healthy lifestyle, it has been agreed that we can sign you off from this hospital trust. You will be able to continue your care with your own GP." This was delivered with smiling enthusiasm.

Caught up in the moment I smiled back. *This was good wasn't it?* I thought about my Mom whose post breast cancer care for a 2cm lump had continued for seven years. I was a star patient, an exception. I mean, it's common knowledge that cancer patients usually receive at least five years care after diagnosis, *isn't it?*

While I processed the questions racing through my head, Miss Khan stood and came around the desk to me, opening her arms for a hug. Rather than voice my concerns, I rose also and thanked her. This was excellent news, *wasn't it?* Eleven months post-surgery and I was signed off from consultant care. No more hospital visits.

"Is there anything you want to ask me before you leave?"

The exit was looming. My cancer adventure was almost over but despite the myriad of questions that filled my head, only one came to the surface.

"Is there a possibility my cancer is hereditary only my father had kidney disease and I underwent several tests as a child?"

The consultant said this was unlikely and reached into a folder, presenting me with a booklet entitled, Kidney Cancer – The Facts.

"Have a flick through this, it should answer most concerns and we're always her if you need us."

I was confused. Did her department operate a helpline? As she walked me to the door my brain was scrambled with unanswered questions, but I remained tongue tied, smiling inanely back at this pleasant woman. But instead of standing my ground, I allowed her to steer me through the open door. As it closed behind me, I felt a mixture of elation and fear. That was it. I was leaving kidney cancer behind, a series of notes and scans in a brown folder on the desk of a woman I barely knew. Who barely knew me.

As I drove home, I thought about what I'd tell Jay and the girls.

"Good news, I now have no consultant and no more hospital care." It was beginning to sink in, was this really progress? I'd not even reached into my pocket for the carefully compiled list of questions; the back-pain issues, abdominal discomfort, did I have nerve damage? I hadn't queried the continued numbness around my scarring. Why do I need answers to these when I have the knowledge that my cancer has gone? I should be elated, proud, shouting from the rooftops.

"I've been discharged from cancer care before twelve months has passed. I am a survivor." Why instead was doubt still gnawing away at me? I felt like a coward all over again.

The fact was I'd wanted to trust her. I'd needed to recover some dignity. Changing hospital was going to be a fresh start, clean slate, wipe out the bad experience and begin again with professionals who cared about me and would deliver the care I needed. Instead I'd had the door close behind me. I was out.

As the festive season was upon us again Jay and I arranged to meet up with Laura and Thomas. Since my surgery, our regular meet ups for a drink had been replaced by going out for coffee or a bite to eat. This evening however we decided to take a walk into the town centre for a drink. First though I wanted their opinion on my hospital gown design.

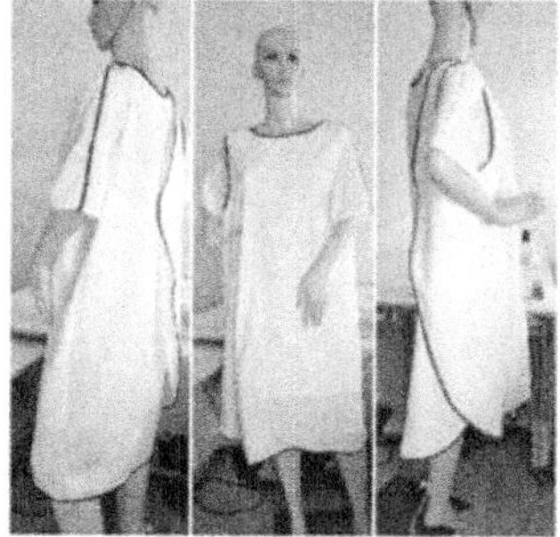

Both having worked as nurses and still NHS professionals they were extremely interested, and Thomas was more than willing to model. The sample gown I'd made was from fabric I'd taken from my stock, a bright African design so not your usual NHS generic print. They were both impressed with how the gown wrapped over requiring no fastenings, the simplicity coupled with its dignity saving design was my USP

Whether it was the excitement of my new venture or a case of drowning my sorrows after being dismissed from hospital care, I drank more than I should have. The company was good, we were out and about and having one too many for the road used to be the norm. Coupled with having taken painkillers though and my lightweight drinking status it most definitely wasn't a good idea. The walk home took twice as long with Jay having to prop me up most of the way. Within sight of the house I tripped and fell, ripping the knee of my jeans, I was a complete state! Once inside I have no idea how Jay got me upstairs, I have a faint recollection of curling up next to Finn in his basket before being led to my own bed.

The following morning, I woke early with a hellish hangover and that feeling of shame that accompanies excess alcohol. My comedown was dramatic. I sobbed and cursed myself for being so stupid. The thought I could have damaged my poor kidney filled me with guilt and I swore that was the last drop of alcohol I'd ever take. Jay was remarkably sympathetic given that I'd rounded a pleasant evening off in such a state and woken in an even worse way. It did wake me up to the fact that I wasn't the party girl I once was so hairdo's and wardrobe choices weren't the only parts of my life that were being toned down. Would I ever dance on a table again or do impromptu Irish jigs in a bar? Could I stay out till the sun came up drinking and singing as we used to and still cope with a fry up for breakfast? Would it be the end of the world if not?

CHAPTER 37 THE ANNIVERSARY OF DISCONTENT

What struck me most when I looked back to March 13th, 2013 was that I didn't seem to have any concept of how serious my condition was. Despite the agonising pain, I was more concerned about leaving the house in pyjamas and the thought of an ambulance pulling up outside the house seemed completely OTT.

I had remained in denial for quite some time. Now that date had come around again, the emotions I felt were coming back to the surface, but I was still trying to push them down. If I were to voice my feelings, there would be a lot of resentment. Not the 'why me' kind of indignation. Shit happens as the saying goes, the chances of any of us getting cancer are 2-1 It was the imbalance within cancer funding and research that I'd witnessed first-hand that vexed me. All cancer patients should have access to the same resources but so many are left behind and kidney cancer patients are high on that list. Cancer inequality had reared its ugly head and the discontentment I felt would not go away.

Being in the cancer club had made me look at people differently. There is no way of knowing if the person next to you in a supermarket queue, on a train or in the cinema has a cancer diagnosis. We don't all look gaunt and thin or wear headscarves and many are still working and making the most of their lives. I had been introduced to kidney cancer patients who, despite metastasis in parts of their body, still ran marathons!

I hadn't expected to be dealing with associated pain twelve months on and it was a constant reminder. I needed to let go of the fear and move on but there was deeper pain inside that hadn't been addressed and I didn't know what to do with it. I had to make a change and getting a new look had always worked for me, it was a start.

I'd regularly reinvented myself, especially my hairstyles. How I looked was reflected in my work and as that was bold and fun, my appearance was pretty 'out there'. I had no wish to get my dreads put back in – they were in a bag in the drawer under my bed just in case I changed my mind. The Mohican had been a good look but was totally impractical when I was taken into hospital. Now I wanted something completely different and as I have never been a follower of mainstream fashion, it had to set me apart from the norm. A perm! That was it, a big curly perm. Back in the late eighties, early nineties I used to go to a guy in town for my perms, he always got it exactly right. Lee was still in business, so I booked an appointment, he was delighted. He didn't get to do many perms now, only the occasional elderly lady and they were very tame. By the time he'd finished with me I had a proper afro! It was perfect. This was how to mark twelve months cancer free, a new hairdo, a fresh start.

On the day of my cancer anniversary or cancerversary as I've heard it called, I took a trip into Birmingham with my friend Fi. This is a trip we used to make regularly, collecting fabric for our respective businesses. Since deciding to reinvent my business, I had been back with Fi to our old stomping ground, Birmingham Rag Market a couple of times. Having been a regular customer for more than fifteen years we know the traders well and I had to explain my absence to a few of them. It made me realise how valued I was not only as a customer, but a friend and I was overwhelmed by the kindness shown to me. On my cancerversary though we decided to have a walk around town and behave like shoppers rather than a workday. We wandered in and out of shops we'd usually never have time for but still chose our usual meal venue, Baguette du Monde and sat on the steps of Victoria Square eating our lunch and taking selfies. It was a perfect way to begin again, not quite starting where I left off, but I was moving towards a new normality and looking forward, not back.

I'd firmly re-established myself back on Twitter and happened to notice a competition to win tickets to see Prince in concert. I'd been a Prince fan since my late teens having heard a session on Radio 1 of his Dirty Mind album and I was hooked. I followed Prince's career through every different stage, he was also a chameleon, changing his look and sound to suit his ever-changing mood. Having seen him in concert several times before, I didn't want to miss an opportunity for a freebie, so I entered and I won! The competition was run by a Birmingham newspaper and I received a call from a reporter asking if I'd answer a few questions so they could do a feature, I obliged.

I was asked how long I'd been a Prince fan, had I been to many concerts, which were my favourite tracks, all the usual questions. Then came the stinger.

"We see from your Twitter bio that you've written a blog, you're a cancer survivor?"

Oh, that. Yes, but it was nothing to do with my Prince fandom. The conversation continued with a myriad of questions about my cancer experience and what I thought of the aftercare. Did I think more awareness should be raised and how would I go about that? I explained I was reluctant to comment on my own experience and reiterated that it had nothing to do with the competition win. The reporter said she understood, it was simply another angle for them to look at. She said not to worry, the piece she'd write would be about my relationship with Prince and his music and the excitement of winning tickets. Do you trust a reporter?

The answer is no. When the paper was published, the article had the header, 'Cancer Survivor Wins Tickets to See Pop Idol Prince!' I couldn't catch my breath. That was exactly what I didn't need when I was trying to put the experience firmly behind me. It could be argued that they'd given an apt description of me. It was after all there to see in my blog which was linked to my Twitter bio. However, this was different, it wasn't about cancer it was about Prince. I wanted to party not remain in the shadow of that hateful disease.

Jay had been to several Prince concerts with me before, but this time offered the second ticket to my friend Claire, another big Prince fan. Travelling over we speculated about where we would be seated as I was a competition winner. Would we be front row, maybe get backstage? On arrival at the venue we collected the tickets and discovered the seats were way up at the back. Claire did laughingly suggest she pretend to be my carer to wheedle our way nearer the front as I was a poor 'cancer victim'. I politely declined!

As Prince concerts go, it wasn't the best we'd seen by a long way. Prince performances had always contained so much energy, he was a dynamo on stage, filling every bit of space. That night he hardly moved from one spot on the stage and although musically he was incredible, the spark had gone from his performance. In retrospect the writing was on the wall, he wasn't well and little did we know that in a few short years he would leave us for good. A victim of pain and the drugs he took to kill it that eventually took his life.

We still enjoyed the show and were thankful for the opportunity to see our idol, the last chance we would get. It was just a shame that my cancer had overshadowed the joy I felt in receiving the tickets. What I'm going to say next may sound controversial but, cancer sells. It sells newspapers, clothes, tickets to events, art, music, etc. You stick the cancer or charity tag on what you need to sell and bingo, publicity and, depending on what you're offering, you sell goods that may not have got the marketing boost that cancer can attract. It grabs attention because we've all been affected by it in some way. I suppose if charities receive much needed funds it doesn't matter how the money comes in or how the publicity is raised.

Maybe focus should be more about the charity than the individual, business or product. In the same way that heart disease is displayed on cigarette packets, cancer is not nice. It's drips and drains, cannulas and catheters and some of us can't shake this association and therefore put the disease and the charity before the associated 'product' whatever that be. Dedicated charities both local and national need our help and the best way to do this is by giving, whether time, money, care, publicity or goods but most importantly not for profit.

I am more than a cancer survivor, kidney cancer does not define me. However, I have learnt a difficult lesson, this disease is going to stay with me for good. No matter how hard I try to ignore it, dismiss it, shake off the shadow it's there sticking like glue. They may have removed the tumour, but the cancer remains, it's stamped me and marked me out.

CHAPTER 38 DEMON DRUGS

In June 2014, Ruby entered Race for Life; a series of fundraising events organised by Cancer Research UK. Ruby chose to run a 5K course around Sutton Park, Birmingham and raised £135 for the charity. Although I didn't join in, I was tempted, especially when we cheered Ruby past the finish line, it was such a wonderful achievement. The participants are each sent a race pack which includes their number and a sign you can pin onto your front or back, putting the name of a person you wish to run for. Some people race in memory of loved ones, others to support friends and family fighting cancer, Ruby wore 'I Race for Life for My Momma' on her back. I was so proud of her; Joey would also have run but was working that day and couldn't swap the shift; she had raced a couple of years before and loved every minute.

I decided that day to apply to run the following year, it would be a target to work towards.

In October 2014 I began running with Jay, he'd taken up running several months previously and I felt the time was right to attempt more physical exercise. It had been over thirty years since I'd last ran, I'd been a keen runner at school and joined the local athletics club focussing on 800m. I managed to get chosen for the County team and probably would have gone further had it not been for peer pressure (which included Benson & Hedges and Merrydown cider).

I really can't remember running again after that unless you count the kid's parents' race at school which was more wrestling than running. Oh, and I did win a tee shirt from O'Neills Bar some years previous for being fastest from the bar to the shoe shop opposite and back – not one of my finer sporting moments.

My first tentative outing with Jay was a mile-long course down a country lane nearby. The weather was perfect and there was no-one else around. As I set off, I felt exhilarated. The sun shone as we ran down the peaceful lane surrounded by beautiful countryside. My trainers beat time on the stony ground and my heart sounded strong in my chest as I breathed the clean air, I felt stronger than I had in months. Having kept myself relatively fit, walking daily I managed the mile distance without issue and was happy to turn and run back. I wasn't about to break any speed records and two miles is hardly a major running achievement but to me it was world beating. The weird thing was that I felt more comfortable running than on a brisk walk. I'm not sure if that was to do with the way running propels you forwards, the natural bounce of your foot, but I didn't feel any ill effects from running, I was enjoying it.

My world had been turned on its head, I could still run. For two miles I had refocused my mind on putting one foot in front of the other and breathing. The back pain niggled but it wasn't stopping me, if anything it hurt more when I got back into the car, sitting was always more uncomfortable.

I was still taking Gabapentin and on occasion when the pain was at its worst, I also had Tramadol. The discomfort spread around my side and under my ribs with the addition of sharp jabbing pains. For this reason, the doctor arranged a chest X-ray and MRI scan. He discovered when booking these that my routine 12-month CT scan had been overlooked. This would normally have been arranged by the consultant under whose care I should have been. The GP also made me an appointment with a specialist at the Royal Orthopaedic Hospital in Birmingham. There is no doubt that I have a very proactive and caring doctor who more than made up for the lack of consultant care.

The MRI scan came first, I'd previously had CT scans, so this was new to me and not at all what I was expecting. I presumed it would be like the CT scan, lie on the bed and be fed through the all-seeing donut. What I hadn't banked on was the noise. The radiologist did explain before I went into the scanner but when it kicked off and the high-pitched buzzing and clanking began, I became ridiculously nervous. A voice came through the microphone in the scanner asking me if I was ok as I appeared to be fidgeting. I thought the machine was going to explode! They had to begin again and I felt totally embarrassed when it was over.

I received the results during the visit to the Orthopaedic Hospital. Thankfully, the scan showed nothing irregular other than what is termed 'wear and tear.' It was explained to me once more how, whilst on the operating table, my body would have been twisted and turned to get the kidney out. This was made more difficult by the haemorrhage that had caused the organ to stick inside me. I reckon I can live with wear and tear after all that.

The specialist asked about the pain medication I was on and raised his eyebrows at the mention of Gabapentin. "That's the Devil's drug." He commented.

When I questioned this, he suggested that a more holistic approach to my pain would be beneficial to both my back and my remaining kidney.

"Has no one suggested yoga?"

I explained how my GP had referred me for more physio which he agreed was well overdue and should have been sorted after my surgery. Hearing that I was currently without any specialist cancer or urology care also came as a shock to him. I knew it had to be wrong.

In January of the New Year 2015 my physiotherapy referral came through which was the biggest revelation of all. The physio asked me to stand up straight and still as she measured from the bottom of my ribcage to the top of my hip bone. The left-hand side was significantly shorter than the right! I was wonky!

Post-surgery I had leant over to the left, possibly because of the pain and to protect the wound. This tilt to the left was placing a strain on the right. I was questioned about the amount of physio I received in hospital and explained the excruciating experience I'd been put through a day after surgery and which had counted as physiotherapy at the time.

The exercises I was given bore similarity to standard yoga poses and after four sessions I was signed off with the proviso that I enrolled in a yoga class. The physio could see that I was determined to improve my posture, correcting the lopsided gait and committing to any exercise that would speed up this process. Physiotherapy gave me a new lease of life and a way to combat the pain so that I could begin to lessen the dose of Gabapentin.

At that time, I was taking 900mg of Gabapentin for what is known as neuropathic pain which I topped up with Tramadol when necessary. Not the best recipe for a solo kidney. My goal now was to work on correcting my posture and ditching the drugs; I was on a mission.

The real decider came when I damaged my shoulder. I'd been walking out of our back gate when it swung shut and the top bolt hit the back of my shoulder. I'd been wearing a tee shirt and felt it come sharp but didn't examine it afterwards. Later the same day Ruby noticed blood on my tee shirt and when she pulled it back, revealed a large wound surrounded by bruising on my shoulder. The dose of Gabapentin I was on was so strong it had disguised the pain I should have felt. That was it, the drugs had to go.

CHAPTER 39 JUDGEMENT

By March 2015 I was running a nine-minute mile and had completely weaned myself off Gabapentin. I was winning.

March 13th, 2015 came and went. No fanfare no celebration or marking the occasion. It's a day I'd rather forget but of course those memories are hard to shake. However, I had other things to occupy my mind now, like completing a 5K race and I didn't want only to complete, I wanted to compete and be the best I possibly could.

I was now regularly running three times per week and had managed the 5K distance, I was working to improve my times. We booked a week away in April to Wales but a week before we went, I found a lump in my breast. I didn't worry too much but due to my Mom's history knew I'd better get it checked. I managed to get an appointment a couple of days before we left with a lady GP and she confirmed what I felt, booking me in for a mammogram the following week.

"I'm away on holiday though," I explained.

"Well, we'll need you to go as soon as you return," she warned and moved the appointment to the following week.

I struggled with whether to tell Jay or not. I didn't want him to worry, especially on our week away but I knew he would see through me and so gave him the news as light-heartedly as I could.

"I'm sure it's nothing," I smiled. "These scans are precautionary, nothing to worry about." Jay was more worried that I'd almost not told him and asked me never to keep anything like this from him. I promised.

We arrived at our remote holiday bungalow on a beach in north Wales and it was breathtakingly beautiful. The sea lapped gently on the shore which lay only a couple of hundred yards in front of our holiday home. Behind and on either side rose the Snowdonia mountain range, it was idyllic.

I hadn't slept well for a few nights, unusual for me as I was normally asleep within minutes of climbing into bed. No matter how much I tried to push thoughts of my forthcoming breast cancer screening away, they crept back – mostly in the dead of night. Therefore, I hoped being away from everything, that I would get a decent night's rest.

I hadn't touched alcohol for a while, it wasn't a conscious decision, I think I just got out of the habit. I'd become a real lightweight in the drinking stakes and the few occasions I'd attempted since my cancer, the hangovers had been horrendous. I was therefore more partial to fruit juice than Merlot and a far cheaper date. The combination of being on holiday and not having slept well led me to make a bad decision. It wouldn't hurt to try a couple of glasses of wine, would it? I'd brought along some wishy-washy wine which I was sure I could handle.

Ugh! It must've been the third glass, but I woke with an awful headache at 3.30am. I did manage to get back to sleep for a while but 5.30am and I was in the wide-awake club with my mind in overdrive and my head pounding. Back on the wagon!

We'd woken to another beautiful sunny day and with nothing to do and nowhere to go, the mini hangover was easy enough to shake off. Walks on the beach with the dogs, exploring the local lanes which lead towards the mountains and simply sunbathing took my mind (and headache) elsewhere.

Running had become my favourite way to relieve stress and put my mind in order and our holiday location had the most scenic courses.

It was a spectacular setting, a straight, flat footpath leading along the coast road with mountains ahead and the sea to the right. At sunrise when we set out most days, the sky was almost clear and each day promised another scorcher, not your average April weather.

The mountains that lay ahead of us were known as the Three Sisters and their colours changed with the rising sun as shadows fell further away from their slopes. Turning at the next village to head back, the sea came in from the right, a scattering of farms with their patchwork fields were in view and the birds attempted to drown out the incoming tide with their dawn chorus.

Running brought all things into perspective. I was feeling good, in the most beautiful surroundings and there was absolutely nothing to fear. How could there be, this was the life.

The week passed far too quickly and on the last day, as I woke and lay listening to the waves gently lapping over the pebbles, I felt incredibly sad. Sad to be leaving and scared of what I may face on my return. As we packed, the wind picked up outside and heavy rainclouds began rolling over the mountains making the sea darker, moodier. I love the elements and took a final walk out across the beach. It was exhilarating, I felt so alive with the sea roaring, wind against me and rain on my face mingled with tears. I was not going through that torment again.

We drove home through the mountains, so we'd get to travel past Snowdonia. The weather didn't improve; wild, wet and windy but it added to the atmosphere conjured up by the magical scenery.

Arriving home, the first thing I saw was a pile of post on the stairs, one letter stood out with its NHS post mark. I put it to one side and began sorting, unpacking and preparing for the week ahead; I knew exactly what I was facing but didn't want to face it there and then. It would be there in the morning.

As the appointment day approached my superstitions began messing with my mind. I couldn't pass a magpie without greeting it and all of its family and friends. The usual triggers were avoided; walking on cracks, going under ladders etc but then there were the made up ridiculous rituals that drove me crazy. Only cooking with even numbers; two onions, six mushrooms, four potatoes etc, use three carrots and something's bound to go wrong, right? Never turning inside out clothes the right way round, asking for trouble. Making sure the volume on the radio or TV is an even number, touching every other lamp post on the way home, I could go on, but they only get more bizarre.

Appointment day arrived but it wasn't until later in the afternoon and, as Joey had a day off, she offered to take me over to the District Hospital for the mammogram.

The Breast Care Unit is a dedicated building for breast cancer patients and the clinic I was attending was a 'New Patient Clinic.' The room soon filled up and with statistics being one in eight women having breast cancer it's apparent that many would leave that day with bad news.

It was weird being back there because it was where I took my Mom for her appointments when she had breast cancer 6 years previous. I also felt as though judgement was being served on me as I'd moaned about the fact that there is so much more dedicated care and fundraising given to breast cancer than other lesser known cancers.

That said I can't fault the NHS, or the level of care given, the appointment was fast tracked and the staff efficient and caring.

I was first called in to see the consultant who, asked to examine me, confirmed the lump and said that he could also feel my lymph nodes were swollen. The first time this happened was two weeks before my kidney cancer introduced itself, so I wasn't happy to hear they were enlarged again. However, my lymph nodes had reappeared since with no sinister consequences so hopefully it was nothing to worry about. He took some more information from me and then sent us back to the waiting room.

Next, I was taken in for a mammogram which wasn't easy given my 32AA size. However, it was done swiftly by two lovely radiographers and I was then taken for an ultrasound scan of the area. For this there were two nurses and a doctor who had a look at the mammogram images then started to scan me. Thankfully, she very quickly confirmed that the lump I had felt was a benign cyst. It was said in a matter-of-fact way, but the relief was immense until she asked the nurses to look at the images explaining that she wasn't happy with what she could see. After some intense re-examination of my boobs it was agreed I'd have to have another mammogram!

Back out to the waiting room, Joey was becoming concerned as I'd been a while in there. I explained what I'd been told and we waited, flicking through the magazines, not voicing our fears. Once the room was free again, I was called for a second mammogram for which I was pushed this way and that like a contortionist holding bizarre positions. Then the radiographers accompanied me in to have another ultrasound. Lying there with five professionals querying what they saw made me incredibly nervous. Then the doctor said I should look, it appeared as though my upper right side was shadowy compared to the left. When they zoomed right in it looked as though I had several other cysts. I was asked to get dressed and sent back out into the waiting room until I could see the consultant again.

Having learnt my lesson about wearing ridiculous clothing when attending hospital I'd attempted to take the lead from Lisanne Vos, another kidney cancer patient who wrote in her blog, R U Kidneying Me about how she turned up for her surgery in gym gear with a positive mental attitude. For this appointment I looked like I'd arrived for a yoga class in leopard print Puma leggings and a fitted sports top – not easy to peel on and off for each examination, another hospital clothing fail.

When I was called back in to see the consultant he got straight to the point, saying the good news was that my lump was benign. He then went on to add that given my history and the fact my lymph nodes were swollen and the ultrasound scan uncertainty he was booking me in for a CT scan.

This was something I'd avoided for a while after having three CT scans plus a bone scan in close succession. However, I felt quite relieved. I only wanted to know if there was anything nasty lurking around inside me and so the saga continued.

I had thought I'd got this cancer thing sorted but it had other ideas. Last time it arrived without warning, this latest scare had taken up the best part of a month and taught me I have no control over that C word. It can torment your head, attack your body, stop you from sleeping and worst of all, keep you guessing.

CHAPTER 40 THE BIG REVEAL

The date was 8th May 2015 and my destination once again was the District Hospital to have a CT scan. I had visited this unit with my Mom before but it was a first for me at that hospital. I hadn't long booked in when I was called to go for blood tests, as usual they needed to make sure my lonesome kidney was functioning well and could cope with the dye I was going to have pumped through me.

Next I was seated in the scan waiting area and given a bottle of water with an iodine solution to drink which apparently helps to show up 'hollow areas.' I had an hour to drink this, taking small sips every ten minutes. The time passed quickly listening to various stories of why other patients were there.

It amazes me how candidly complete strangers sit discussing their most personal medical conditions with each other. Before I'm halfway down my bottle of water I've been regaled with tales of malfunctioning colostomy bags and heard a debate as to which type of hernia pain is worst. When the topic of surgery scars arises I grab a magazine to read and make sure I don't make eye contact with anyone or worse still get an impromptu eyeful of scar tissue as they take it in turns lifting tops and pulling down waistbands.

By the time I'm called for my scan I'm desperate for a wee but not allowed to go, this explains why everyone who has exited the scanning room heads straight for the toilet, it is not easy on your bladder. I forget to ask but presume my kidney is doing ok as they prepared to insert the canular in my arm.

CT scans don't require you wear a gown as long as your clothing doesn't have any metal on it so I'm in leggings and a vest top. Once on the scan bed I start shivering and so I'm offered a blanket. Only my arm is out for the venflon to be inserted and then both arms must be raised above my head.

The first time I was fed into the machine was without dye and I heard the familiar 'breathe in and hold it.... now breath out' as the whirring tunnel took me through. After a couple of goes I was out again on the conveyor and the radiographer put the dye through the venflon and reminded me of the sensation of weeing. I was secretly praying that wasn't the case because the sensation was so real and my bladder was fit to burst. Another couple of goes and I was back out and could climb from under my blanket and head for the loo.

As I left I got the nods and smiles from those still waiting and a couple of 'hope all is ok's' which was when I started thinking less about my bladder and more about why I was there. *Please let it be ok.*

I felt so pathetic as I was unable to wait for more than a week before phoning the secretary in the radiology department for any news. An extremely sympathetic secretary explained that she'd speak to the consultant and get back to me. Good to her word I received a call back soon after to say I'd got an all clear. No fuss, no excuses, there was real empathy at work in this department and they delivered the best news I could have in the nicest possible way. Throughout this latest cancer related ordeal, the treatment had been second to none, proof that it doesn't have to be so bad.

I draw another line under cancer and begin again.

PART THREE RUNNING FOR MY LIFE

CHAPTER 41 TALKING THE PLANK

Pre kidney cancer I would say I was relatively fit. Not long before my tumour was discovered I had been on a mission to improve my health and wellbeing generally. Jay and I had always walked regularly and I was clocking up several miles a day. Back then I thought yoga was a gentle exercise and not worth the effort and that going to a gym was out of the question. The only time I'd entered a fitness suite was for one of those tums and bums classes for toning up after I'd had the girls. It was a disaster, after a few minutes of intense jumping around I was so out of breath the instructor thought I was having an asthma attack. She seated me at the back and aimed a fan at me! Rather than go through that humiliation again I began doing a few exercises at home, these included the plank; getting into a push up position on the floor, holding for a set time (the longer the better) and slowly lowering your body down in a straight line from shoulders to ankles.

The night before I was taken ill, I had been on a decent walk and returned to do a few exercises and when it came to the plank, I had pushed that bit further, holding for two minutes. I can't remember feeling any differently and in truth wouldn't know for sure that this was what kicked off the bleed but, in the absence of any other explanation it's a decent guess.

So many times I've asked the question, why did it bleed? Doctors have said there's no solid explanation, but they haven't dismissed that by pushing myself that bit further in the dreaded plank it may have done me a favour, alerting me to the cancerous invader within.

Following the advice from both my GP and the physiotherapist, I decided it was time to give yoga a go. I researched local classes and was recommended one that had a weekly session in a gym on an industrial estate. Once again, my sidekick, Fi accompanied me – I'm not sure I'd have been brave enough alone.

A bit wiser after the failed Pilates class, we had both invested in decent leggings and loose-fitting tee shirts, no fashion statements. The business we'd chosen was Midlands Yoga and it was run by a lovely young lady, Gemma. We warmed to her immediately, there were no yogic pretentions and it wasn't cliquey. Gemma and the class were welcoming and friendly and we were able to blend easily into the back of the class.

My limited yoga research and preconceptions led me to believe that the exercises would be steady and relaxing and this, being a beginner's class would be gentle, not at all taxing. What I hadn't bargained on was that one of the poses we'd be asked to strike was the plank. Until that moment I'd virtually forgotten my old exercise regime and hadn't thought much about the plank position I'd held prior to my kidney tumour rupturing. When asked to move into that exercise though I froze. At the start of the class we were advised that if a position is too much for you to curl up in a child's pose; knees underneath torso, head tucked in and arms by your sides. I adopted this, closing my eyes tightly.

It didn't put me off yoga though, on the contrary, when the class moved venue to a local boxing club, Fi and I followed. I'd had a quiet word with Gemma by then about my history, so she was aware of my fears and limitations. Nothing was expected of any of us, I learnt that yoga suits each individual in their own way. Once on the yoga mat, you have your own space, no one judges and the only goals are yours and yours alone. I was loving it and, I was progressing well.

It wasn't long before I could maintain balance in a yoga position for the required time and this was having a positive effect on my posture. I'd even attempted a headstand; something I'd not taken on since childhood when I could watch an entire episode of Blue Peter on my head. I wouldn't make it through an ad break now but at least I was getting up there! Eventually I could hold the plank position without dropping my knees, it was a major achievement and a big step forward in my recovery.

The drive for fitness even extended to playing netball. When my girls set up a team for fun, Fi and I were more than happy to join in (if we didn't have to play against any real netball enthusiasts). I was overcoming my fears about physical exercise and my capabilities. In fact, I was doing more than I'd done since school.

Yoga was no longer pencilled in my diary, it was there in bold and underlined, not to be missed. Next on my to-do list was my business, how to move it forward and get back the passion I once felt for it.

CHAPTER 42 THORN IN MY SIDE

I had been on my way to Central Hospital in Birmingham to have my cancer carrying kidney removed when Thorn in My Side by Annie Lennox began playing on the radio. At that time it was the tumour that ate into me, ruining my life but immediately afterward I turned to my business for blame. Work became the problem, the cause and irritation, the reason I'd been ill and the catalyst for the cancer.

Everything from my home to my appearance had reflected my work, I mirrored Missfit, the business was me. I had been confident and outgoing and could walk the walk as far as the fashionista image went. As the dust settled and my recovery improved, I struggled to shake the negative connotations I associated with Missfit. My lifestyle hadn't helped but I had been living my business and something had to go, not only a kidney.

Each time I'd attempted to kick start the business once more, the feelings of uncertainty would crowd in and I'd lose any enthusiasm I'd mustered. Even my attempt at redesigning and launching a new hospital gown had been filed away again. Missfit had become the thorn in my side and I had to decide once and for all whether to save what was left of it.

So it was that not long after my breast cancer scare, I'd phoned HMRC again and asked to close the business. After the call it wasn't disappointment or sadness that I felt but relief, one less thing to worry about. My website displaying the logo and an outline of the business remained in place, but I removed all items for sale and placed them instead on eBay to sell as a job lot. The majority of stock was vintage clothing, around six hundred items in all and it wasn't long before interest was shown. A woman contacted me and asked to purchase the stock, both vintage and my own pop fashion designs. A fair price was reached and she arrived one day with a van into which my entire business stock was loaded. As I helped carry armfuls of clothes to the van I was holding memories; Clothes Show collections, boy band outfits, vintage menswear popular with Peaky Blinders fans, Kylie Minogue costumes, years of my work disappearing within ten minutes in a Ford Transit off to London. It was over.

No longer would I have to 'rock a look' or 'work a trend.' The dreads were tied in a scrunchie under the bed and my Mohawk long grown out. Cancer hadn't only taken my kidney; it had obliterated my confidence and without that I didn't feel able to carry off the pretence needed to run an alternative fashion business. But what next?

Business may have come to a halt, but my running kept going. I wanted to push my limitations; see how far I could go. That first time back out on the road had felt like a light being switched back on and now I was relishing that feeling of exhilaration when you've reached a target.

Eight months on and I was regularly running three times per week between two and three miles each time and health issues were paling into insignificance. My wardrobe had altered considerably with the beloved Adidas hi-tops being replaced by Asics trainers and I was unashamedly wearing lycra out in daylight. My most essential piece of kit was the water bottle as I'd discovered one kidney meant I needed extra hydration, especially when running longer distances.

In my school days when I was an 800m runner and doing particularly well, I received a wonderful gift from my best friend, Jenni. My maiden name was Florence which led to the nickname Flo and after a particularly good race win Jenni presented me with a tee shirt that had 'Seb Flo' printed on it, Seb Coe being a hero of mine at the time. I text her mentioning my return to running and pointed out I'd increased my distance and therefore may need another tee shirt printing, maybe Flo Farah?

According to plan, I entered Race for Life together with Ruby and on 7th June 2015 we took our places amongst the sea of women in pink to run for Cancer Research UK. While I couldn't wait to get started, Ruby was clearly there for the pre-race warm-up and disco which provides a fun and emotive build up to the main event. We began by jumping around with an overzealous Zumba instructor to up-tempo feel-good tunes until we felt we'd already run 5K. Then the stage was taken by a cancer survivor and the family of a loved one who had lost their battle and we were given an inspirational story to drive us on in our quest to finish the race and raise the vital funds needed.

Although it was quite clearly a charity race and not a competition, I had my sights set on getting a personal best. When the time came to make our way to the starting line, we made a loose arrangement to stay together during the race. It must have been very loose as despite my daughter's dedication in returning to run for me, I left her less than a mile in! A long-forgotten feeling came over me as I ran, I rediscovered my competitive spirit. I was back in the race, picking off other runners as we moved along the wooded paths through Sutton Park. I was fixated on the person in front, pushing hard until I'd caught and overtaken them. I strode past women in pink tutu's and girls wearing glittery fairy wings, I wasn't in a fun run, I was going for a medal. The fact there were no prizes for first, second and third was lost on me. The medals in this race were to celebrate taking part.

Jay was waiting at the finish and said he watched as the first woman ran past the line, closely followed by the second and as he looked at the field of runners coming towards him, to his amazement he saw me. I came tenth out of around 450 runners! He was taken so unaware he hardly had time to get his phone out to take a photo. I was on fire, no stopping me now.

Within the next week I'd applied for another race, this time a real one with no fun in the title. It was the City of Birmingham 10K, I needed to up my distance by half again. I knew it wouldn't be easy, but I'd got the running bug proper. The feeling I got from running was like no other, I was in a zone that outpaced all the negative thoughts in my head, leaving them far behind. If I could keep going, everything would be ok, cancer couldn't catch me. I understood why people say they're running for their life, it's not only a cliché it's a real lifesaver.

Around this time, the James Whale Fund for Kidney Cancer were in the process of rebranding as Kidney Cancer UK. This was the charity I intended to raise funds for. They had joined forces with another kidney cancer charity, Facing Up 2 Kidney Cancer founded by Jon and Sarah Birchall who's fundraising efforts were going towards a research project into the disease. Now I had even more reason to cross that 10K finish line, I couldn't let my sponsors down. It also gave me more purpose; I was running because I've had kidney cancer and not despite it.

CHAPTER 43 UP AND RUNNING

September came around and I got that familiar feeling, the start of something new was dawning. I still bought myself academic diaries, a throwback to years I spent working in school administration. September was the time of year for fresh starts, new beginnings and in my case, a return to work. HMRC were again patient with me and understanding of my situation. With their help Missfit was re-registered and I began looking for new opportunities.

With several hundred images to show from past collections I started by sharing some favourites on social media. I didn't have a plan of action; it was simply to repopulate my accounts and show people I was back in business. Soon after I had a message from a photographer asking to work with me on a pop fashion photoshoot. He thought my designs would fit the genre he wanted to portray, pop meets art in a fun setting. I agreed to work with him.

Despite having sold most of the stock a few months previous, I had kept a large quantity of fabrics and haberdashery. I'd also begun adding to my collection with stretch jerseys and lycra as my interest in activewear had taken over. Amongst these I had some swimwear fabric in shiny red, white and blue stars and stripes. There was also a selection of wet look pvc with neon coloured graffiti and bold prints. These are what I worked with to produce a mini collection for the Alix Heru photoshoot. The images he produced were amazing. Using two female models he had created a mock beach where the girls had brought my designs to life in a cool, artistic way. With maybe the best professional shots I'd ever had, I was now well equipped to showcase my business and reignite some interest. In fact, scrolling through the images he'd sent, maybe the wrong kind of interest... As is the norm with photographer collaborations rather than directing for your sole purpose, you can expect a few more 'artistic' shots. In this case there were a couple of topless photos, well when I say topless that is apart from a few strategically places sweeties!

I'd had a call around this time from my friend Netty who ran a town centre tattoo parlour where I got my own personal artwork designed. During the time spent doing my sleeve the previous year we'd discussed working together on a clothing design, Netty was in the process of working on a degree in textiles and wove her own fabrics. The result was a series of days spent together designing and making a Japanese inspired coat woven from fabric Netty created. It was a work of art which, would go on to win awards at the University of Derby. This further boosted my confidence as far as getting back behind my sewing machine and being creative once more.

My running training was about to be put to the test as in late September I ran my first 10K race. I'd managed the distance on practice runs a few times and was confident I could achieve a decent time for my age group. The event was put on by UK Triathlon so I knew it would be a well organised race and it would be my first experience of chip timing.

The only part of the run that I'd change in hindsight would be my starting position. When more serious runners going for personal best times were asked to move forward, I deliberately moved back in the crowd not wanting to put myself ahead of a 'serious runner.' However, knowing the course as I did, I then found myself having to walk/jog for the first part of the race as there was simply no room which was a frustration.

I didn't do too badly though considering it was my first attempt. Scanning down the results online I saw I was in 53rd place although I prefer the fact I was 14th in my age category. My chip time was 57.39 which didn't beat my personal best of 54.02 but I'd learnt not to hover at the back again. Judging by the finish line photo that Jay took I looked as though I had more to give, appearing to want to fly past with my arms outstretched!

What I learnt from this event was that I was more determined to succeed than I'd imagined. I was now a serious competitor with a medal to prove it. Jay took me for a meal after the race and I insisted on wearing my medal throughout. I'd also managed to raise £1500 for the kidney cancer research project funded by Facing up 2 Kidney Cancer. I'm not sure I'd have taken up running again were it not for my illness, I had a lot to be thankful for.

I now had plenty to repopulate my social media feeds with, apart from the latest photoshoot pics I was sharing my running progress. I'd never been wholly comfortable putting myself in front of the lens, it had been made easier by the business image I portrayed. Without the dreads and crazy clothes though I felt laid bare but knew the importance of sharing part of yourself to gain interest. People like to know who they're buying from, adding a touch of personality to what I created meant showing up now and again in the media feed.

Starting up the business again I made a firm decision not to hide behind anything, to tell it like it was. The fashion industry has a lot of smoke and mirrors, it's not nearly as glamourous as it appears and my situation certainly wasn't. Working from a bedroom with a workshop in the back yard. I didn't want to skim over the reason Missfit had dropped off the catwalk for so long either so I referenced my cancer blog in the business website, it was part of my story now, like it or not.

A scroll down my Instagram feed would now include photos of trainers, leggings, personal best times and running routes. I was hashtag fitgirl! Twitter, my favourite app now followed UKRunchat and daily yoga meditations along with reams of other fitness fans. As my horizons broadened, so did those of my business, opportunities were springing up all over.

Although I still had a personal interest in the alternative and pop fashion market, I barely kept up with latest trends on the catwalk. The clothing I had my eye on more closely was the growing activewear trend. I'd seen a mock-up video from Australia, poking fun at fashion conscious girls wearing their gym gear to shop in, go to work, clean the house, take the kids to school. The message was 'wear activewear anywhere' and hilarious as the send up was, it was a fact. Young women were increasingly wearing yoga leggings and gym tops out and about, it was a growing trend. I'd found my new niche, fun and funky activewear. I could design and make fitness clothing that would look as good on the High Street as on a workout.

I took out a new notepad (essential when starting a fresh business project) and began writing.

Where does my passion now lie? – Health & Fitness

Which part of my business was already set up for this? – Miss'Fit'

What was I waiting for?

I'd spent years explaining to customers 'No I'm not Miss Fit' it's *Missfit* and now, well I kind of was, at least that is I would be selling a range of health and fitness clothing and accessories. I continued jotting down ideas for a range of pop fashion fitness clothing. I also looked at ordering some accessories to stock. It was the new start I'd been waiting for and once again, it had come about because of cancer. Take the positives.

CHAPTER 44 RUNNING FROM CANCER

Thanks to my blog and subsequent fundraising from running, in November of 2015 I was invited to speak at a Kidney Cancer Information Day in Birmingham. The event was being held at a large city centre hotel and hosted by Kidney Cancer UK, formerly the James Whale Fund for Kidney Cancer. A representative from the charity Malcolm, phoned to ask whether I'd consider speaking about my experience as many members were following the blog I wrote. I didn't like to refuse as it sounded as though they really wanted me there. It could be helpful to other patients or carers to hear my story first-hand, so I agreed. I should have thought more about it before saying yes as my blog had not been easy to write. Speaking that experience would be even more difficult as I would soon find out.

The request came at the time I was getting busy with my new business venture. I was making a concerted effort to put a positive spin on the C word and focus on the F word instead, Fitness. Now though I would have to go back in time and voice the events that had led to me putting pen to paper.

The Kidney Cancer Information Day was a turning point. Kidney Cancer UK was the charity that had given me so much advice and support and I was more than willing to help if I could. Malcolm kept in close contact and advised me what would be needed, just a short talk about my own kidney cancer experience and how |I came to write the blog. However, the impact of preparing for and then actually speaking out loud had a profound effect on me.

Rather than give hope or inspire positivity I felt I was bringing the event down. My experience had been – in my opinion, awful and I hoped not common amongst kidney cancer patients. I'd spent some time preparing a shortened account of what I'd been through to read but as I stood in front of the small audience (only around 20 people attended), my mouth dried up and I struggled to find the right words. As I read my notes all I wanted to do was apologise and hope that no-one else had to go through the same. Coming to the end of the piece my voice trailed off, I wanted to cry and when I looked up at the silent audience something amazing happened, they clapped. They applauded enthusiastically and I was faced with genuine concern and understanding.

It was hard to take in and I was left wondering. *"Why are you clapping? What I've just read to you is not how it's meant to be."*

Afterwards, I spoke to some of the patients there, the fact there were so few in attendance made me sad. Despite all the hard work and effort the Fund had put in they didn't seem to get the recognition that some other charities do. Those patients who had been through or were still being treated for kidney cancer each had similar stories of poor care, lack of information, isolation, lack of medication, no access to support etc. A fellow patient there slipped me a piece of paper with the name of another dedicated charity, the Kidney Cancer Support Network. She told me about the woman that ran it, Rose Woodward and urged me to get in touch, it was a charity run by patients, for patients.

When I left the hotel that day I wanted to run, literally run away from my association with kidney cancer. I had an overwhelming feeling of 'what's the point?' I felt guilty for having shared my story rather than pride in getting up there which is why putting it into words has proven so difficult.

This was made even harder by another action I took following the Information Day. If nothing else, one of the pieces of advice I took and followed through from that day was to pursue my medical records. Considering what I'd experienced maybe I'd find answers there.

I had to pay £20 to acquire my medical records and they arrived in a brown manila folder about an inch thick and included two copies of scan discs. The discs could only be read by inserting password data and this information came separately in another envelope. To be honest, I couldn't make head nor tail (nor kidney) of my scan images. I wasn't sure which ones displayed both kidneys; what bit was the tumour or where the gap in my abdomen appeared.

As for the notes, I could write an essay on those findings. I read through them carefully, page by page and was astounded at some of the information or rather misinformation they contained.

Multiple wrong diagnosis recorded, drug administration incorrect, drugs given inadequate, pain levels recorded as zero when at the time they were off the scale and it went on.

One of the most infuriating pages was a letter sent from the consultant to my GP after my surgery which managed to get the size and grade of my tumour wrong despite a histology report to the contrary. It was as though they couldn't be bothered to look at the facts.

The physiotherapist who had watched as I unceremoniously dropped onto another patient's bed in agony had recorded that I'd achieved all goals set 'without problem.' It had even printed the length of my stay after surgery as three days when I was in there for five. My notes were a complete farce. When my girls read through they were astonished at both the misinformation and apparent lack of painkilling drugs administered.

We found the information on my childhood history with kidney disease recorded which wasn't flagged up at any stage of my treatment. The problem was, I had no idea what to do with this or where to go. With no ongoing specialist care there was only my GP to speak to.

My relationship with the word cancer was now at an all-time low. Any positives I'd taken from the experience were diminishing. I felt cheated. I wanted no association with cancer. I hardly ever updated my blog and when I did it was half-heartedly. What was the point? Not only had the hospital care been diabolical, they couldn't even be bothered to write the notes up correctly. In fact, they'd glossed over the worst bits making my stay seem textbook, maybe they had a precedent file which they referred to, copying the data in for every patient.

I was disillusioned with cancer charities in general as well having now experienced the gaping chasm of care that existed within cancer care. There didn't appear to be equal access to funding, support and help in general. Kidney cancer, along with other lesser known types of the disease weren't being dealt with the same gravity as those ranked higher.

When I gave my talk to the Kidney Cancer UK back in November, I'd spoken about an experience I had in a local card shop. When offered the obligatory pen to fund cancer research I was asked to choose between breast or prostate cancer. I asked if there was pen for which profit went to the whole range of cancer research. The woman at the till looked blankly back at me saying, "No, we only do breast and prostate."

I suggested she feedback to the company responsible that there are more than one hundred types of cancer.

"I know," She replied. "You're not the first person to point that out but I can't help you there." Leaning forward she whispered, "We have to push the pens, it's in our job description, I don't agree with it."

I wasn't alone. I knew that but why is there such disparity? Surely cancer is cancer. How come then equal funding for research, treatment and care isn't afforded to all cancer patients. It wasn't fair and to be reminded of that on the High Street, doubly so.

CHAPTER 45 ATONEMENT

With my three-year cancerversary on the horizon and as I'd heard nothing about the scan, I should be due, I rang the hospital to see if I was booked in. Surprise, surprise, the administrator said they had no record of any forthcoming appointments for me. The knock-on effect of having no consultant or ongoing specialist cancer care.

In less than three months we were due to celebrate the wedding of our eldest, Joey to Thomas so preparations were hotting up. None more so than the wedding dress which, I was of course making. What I didn't need now was any extra worries or niggling concerns, I wanted the scan and to hear those words, no evidence of disease before the big day.

As I had the previous year, I would have to speak to my GP to get the scan arranged. I was struggling with what I presumed was a water infection, symptoms of which I was familiar since having only one kidney so I booked in at the surgery. Unfortunately, my GP was away so I had to see a locum. I explained my symptoms and, although I know doctors aren't keen on patients self-diagnosing, I said I was quite sure it was a UTI, I'd had so many. I was surprised therefore when he suggested I'd maybe drunk too much coffee!

"I haven't drunk coffee in three years." I sighed.

"Do you eat a lot of citrus fruit then?" He quizzed.

Seriously? Should I draw his attention to the fact I've got one kidney owing to the other being fished out carrying a large tumour?

I left minus medication and a polite, "See how you go, come back if it gets worse."

I did keep going – to the loo, frequently, painfully until my own GP returned and gave me the antibiotics I needed as well as assuring me he'd sort my annual CT scan.

With the three-year marker looming I was feeling very bewildered. I couldn't fault my GP; he had gone above and beyond what most doctors would. Not only the ongoing care, he understood and empathised with what I had been through, he knew me and that was because he paid attention and listened. So many health care professionals appear not to notice the person in front of them. Maybe it's the hospital gowns, their purpose is to make us faceless, drain our personalities so we all fit neatly into their tick boxes.

I was feeling so despondent that I decided to call the MacMillan Helpline. No matter how many times I slammed the door on cancer, it had a way of prising open a gap, it was there in the corner of my mind. I wanted to speak to a cancer expert, someone who knew the rules. I got quite tearful on the call because she reaffirmed my fears when she said, "You've been signed off, already?"

More questions followed.

"Have you seen a specialist nurse? Were you given a care plan, scan dates, regular kidney function tests etc?"

"No." I answered to each question. "My GP has picked up all the ongoing care."

In fact, I'd had no idea I should have seen a specialist nurse. I'd been on a renal ward, there hadn't been any other kidney cancer patients while I was there, I'd asked. I had so many unanswered questions and they were spilling out.

"Are all cancer patients supposed to get 5-year specialist care?"

"Does kidney cancer differ significantly from other cancer treatments?"

"Should/can children of kidney cancer patients be tested?"

"Does kidney cancer care differ between hospital trusts?"

"Do other kidney cancer patients suffer with ongoing backpain?"

"What caused the large haemorrhage in my kidney/tumour?"

She had to stop me.

"Most of these are questions for a specialist, a kidney cancer specialist and you are entitled to both a consultant and the answers to your questions.

I explained my mistrust of the system, the medical notes I'd paid for, the discrepancies I'd found, page after page. They'd left me with more questions than ever.

We spoke of my continued back pain, newfound fitness regime, how yoga and running were helping not only with my general health but also giving me a new perspective, a better lifestyle. I was progressing, getting on with things, making my own way but I still had an overnight bag tucked away for emergencies and that left the nagging question. Where would I go? More to the point, who would I call?

It felt like a game of chance and I was running out of cards – and hospitals. The MacMillan nurse listened and sympathised, advised and rallied me to pursue consultant care.

"You must return to your GP and ask to be referred. You absolutely should not have been signed off or dismissed, this is totally wrong and unprecedented." I could hear the anger in her voice, she was genuinely concerned. To be fair, my GP had asked if I'd wanted him to sort out another consultant at another hospital, but I'd declined. It was like pass the patient. I felt I wouldn't be welcome anywhere. Why should another specialist feel differently? They all had long patient lists, not enough hours in the day. Send them an extra one with a complex history who's walked away from her first and been dismissed from her second hospital. They'd be delighted. Not.

The call had been useful. I'd had atonement. I wasn't wrong after all. So, what next?

March 13th, 2016 came and went. Nothing changed. Soon after came the anniversary of my Dad's death, it would be 36 years this time. Being only twelve at the time there was so much I'd missed out on; I barely knew him. We never had chance for a grown-up conversation and now more than ever I had so much to ask him. The most pressing question at that time was 'What was wrong with your kidneys?'

I tried various ways to find out about my Dad's medical history but it seemed a futile mission. I approached the NHS Records office; not as easy as you may think. After my third phone call I was put through to a woman who advised me that after twenty-five years, records are destroyed.

I do know that he was hospitalised as a young man with some class of kidney disease. In his thirties he suffered terribly with kidney stones but that's the extent of my knowledge.

My own medical records show that in 1975 and 1977 I have procedures to investigate my kidney function. It's recorded that I had a pyelography, I had to Google this but have a vivid memory of what it entailed. I'm aged about eight and taken to a local hospital as an outpatient by my Mom. I'm not sure exactly how but, I was pumped full of liquid (I've a sneaking suspicion I remember where the tube went in!) I can recall looking down at my tummy and it seemed massive. I'm told to hold my bladder for some time before being allowed to wee into a large bowl. I remember feeling embarrassed and ashamed as well as confused. Not half as confused as I am now looking back on it as I've no idea why or what the findings meant. The only two words printed after this were Kidney Disease. What am I supposed to make of that forty years on and minus one kidney? So far, both consultants I've met have dismissed this information saying they bear no relevance to my current condition. This annoys me as, having two daughters myself, what if there are hereditary factors. If there's even the slightest risk, I want to know.

Unfortunately, as far as my Dad's medical history goes, I've met a dead end, literally.

CHAPTER 46 THIRD TIME LUCKY

After a lengthy discussion with my GP about the way forward with my care, I agreed to another referral. This time with the University Hospital, Birmingham. The reputation of this hospital is well known, it's got the biggest critical care unit in Europe, the sheer size of the hospital makes it appear more like a town than a medical centre when viewed from afar. I knew little about the urology department there but what I did know of the hospital was its excellent worldwide reputation. Surely this meant third time lucky?

It was a tough decision to go back into the system with another consultant and I felt incredibly apprehensive. I had so many unanswered questions but would they want to take me on? I already felt rejected and overlooked, what if this next consultant didn't want to add to his patient list, would I be a burden?

Rather than relief at getting back on the radar I felt dread and that made me sad.

Before I made it to my appointment at the University Hospital I was referred once more to the District Hospital where there was a Breast Care Unit as I had more lumps. I went back through the procedure of examination, mammogram and ultrasound to be told I had a cluster of cysts. In amongst the cluster was a rogue lump that had the radiologists guessing. I lay in the ultrasound room, my boobs covered in gel, radiologists, nursing staff and eventually a doctor who was summoned, all looking at the screen as the probe was pressed into my chest. My heart was pounding so much it's a wonder it didn't show on the scan. It seemed to take ages before the doctor confirmed it was another cyst and I could leave.

In April 2016 I arrived at the University Hospital, Birmingham with Ruby to meet my new consultant. I felt a little like a naughty child being given a last chance before I was expelled for good.

After a two hour wait, by which time I was feeling sick with nerves, we were called in.

The first thing I noticed was that there were two other nurses present in the room, one of which was a uro-oncology nurse specialist. This is the first time I'd seen a specialist nurse in three years, I hadn't realised they existed at the other hospitals and only found out about them thanks to Macmillan.

The consultant led a quickfire Q&A which was a little awkward as I really didn't want to speak about my previous experience, I wasn't there to complain. It was established that the hospital protocol stated that I should have received regular CT scans for 2 years and continuing ultrasound scans for the remaining 3 years giving a full 5-year remission period. Therefore, I was booked to have a CT scan as soon as possible so they could assess what was happening before continuing care.

I asked about my family history, my Dads kidney problems, my Aunt's death from kidney cancer and my own health record having kidney disease on it. I was told that this wasn't relevant right now and that a CT would be needed to help determine any issues.

We discussed any other ongoing health concerns but again the scan would be necessary to see if there were any underlying problems. I also mentioned the back pain I've suffered with since surgery and he did say this could be nerve damage and therefore he would refer me to a pain management specialist. Again, this was a first as at Central I was told it had nothing to do with the surgery even though I'd had no pain before it.

The nurse specialist took notes throughout and when we were leaving came out with me to further reassure us of what would now follow. I was sent from there to have a blood test to see if my kidney was functioning properly. The nurse gave me a copy of the notes outlining what had been said as well as a leaflet about the service and a holistic questionnaire to fill in. She was wonderful and made me feel a whole lot better.

It was a far better experience than any I'd had previously. As well as an introduction to a nurse specialist it was the first time I'd received any kind of leaflet from a hospital in 3 years. I welcomed pain management as I didn't want to remain on medication indefinitely and being up to date with appointments and scans would also be a relief.

Soon after my appointment at the University Hospital I received a date for a chest X-Ray which would be followed by a renal ultrasound. There was also a scan of my bladder requested. These had all be arranged by my GP prior to meeting the consultant.

At the beginning of May we celebrated Joey's wedding to Thomas, I made the wedding dress of course as well as most bridesmaid's dresses. I was therefore featured in many images appearing on social media via a variety of accounts. I noted that I needed to practice my, 'being caught unaware face' as there were several unflattering candid photos. Thank goodness radiology departments don't have a Facebook page, I'm not sure my chest and abdomen would attract as many likes.

My next appointment with the camera was for the CT scan booked through the University Hospital. I'm sent to the District Hospital as it's nearer my home which helps. Unfortunately, the spray tan I'd invested in for the wedding was still visible. I'd been instructed by my daughters on how to moisturise and exfoliate but two weeks after I looked like I had huge freckles on my torso.

Once more I was directed to a cubicle where I changed into another washed out hospital gown. Sitting back in the waiting room I realised the fading tan made it look as though I hadn't washed for months. It dawned on me as I watched the red lights above the scanning rooms flash on and off that the last time I had arrived there was on a stretcher. The District Hospital is where the tumour was discovered. I recalled being wheeled in, past waiting patients and taken directly into a scan room. They do have a machine next to the Emergency Department, but it was in use. In my mind's eye I saw the route via lengthy corridors, watching the strip lights above me. I heard the voices talking over me, hushed so as not to alarm. Now, in control, I could walk in and out myself. So why did I feel terrified once more?

I'm called in and it's another trip through the tunnel for the scan I should have had over twelve months ago had I not been wrongly discharged. It will be the sixth scan/X-ray in two months, talk about making up for lost time. I know the drill well by now and nod as I'm given instructions by the radiology nurse. The scan bed feeds me into the tunnel and the machine whirrs into action then stops. The bed is reversed back out and the radiologist himself appears next to me.

"I'm sorry, we're picking something unusual up on your side." He said, "can I just check?" He motioned to my waist. I nodded and he felt down the right side of me, my kidney side. "Ok that's fine", he smiled. "Sometimes the scanner can pick up odd shadows."

Odd shadows? I'm not convinced.

When I return home I find a letter inviting me for a further renal ultrasound! I phone and explain I'm just back from a CT and they agree to stand me down. There can't be much of me that doesn't appear on film now.

Whilst I'm grateful for the sudden burst of interest being shown in my chest and abdomen, there's always the fear that something nasty will turn up on the images. There is bliss in ignorance after all. I need to delete Facebook again!

After a three week wait, I receive a letter from the University Hospital giving me all the clear from the CT scan. Relief is an understatement as I was beginning to have doubts. I'm optimistic generally but the ongoing pain had knocked my confidence. Also, the 'odd shadow' that appeared at my side didn't instil me with confidence. Whatever it was, it didn't show up in my results. Finally, I've crossed the three-year line with a definitive all clear!

CHAPTER 47 PAIN MANAGEMENT

Only one month on and I got the appointment through to see the pain management specialist, someone I should probably have seen at least two years ago. Despite the ongoing yoga exercises, the pain in my back and abdomen was still evident and showed up frequently in sharp jabbing pains under my ribs. Despite having stopped taking the Gabapentin pain killing drugs, the pain was winning again and at its worst, I relented although I hated the thought of side effects.

I was beginning to think they were also mind numbing. Getting back to work, my creativity had been stilted. I'd put much of my reticence to return to the job down to my life changing experience, taking a high dose of these drugs couldn't have helped though.

The diagnosis of nerve damage had never been conclusive which is why the latest scans had left me feeling anxious, what if something more sinister was causing the pain? Then again, not having taken much more than paracetomol for a hangover prior to kidney cancer, what if the drugs were doing me more harm than good? After all, my lone kidney needed to filter them.

Another reason I'm alarmed is that I hear a case of a young girl who's jumped out of a bedroom window thinking she would float down. She didn't, multiple bones were broken. The reason for her blind confidence was Gabapentin. Apparently, they are an extremely popular prescription medication and can enhance the effects of other banned substances like opiates. This misuse has led to a reclassification of the drug to class C making it illegal to possess without a prescription.

A couple of weeks prior to the pain management appointment I decide to stop taking the Gabapentin again but, unlike previously when I slowly lessened the dose, I simply stopped. Bad move. For about a week I felt so poorly, extremely low, you know that awful end of the world feeling you get after a bad hangover? If this was cold turkey, I don't want to take drugs ever again. I found out that these are common side effects and realised I'd only got myself to blame. By the time the pain appointment came around I'd been off Gabapentin a little over 2 weeks, I was taking co-codamol instead so not entirely drug free. The appointment was back at the University Hospital which I decided to travel to by train as the nearest station is a short walk along a path from the hospital.

While waiting to go in I was given some Q&As to fill in about my pain which involved answering questions on a scale of 1-10. How bad the pain became in differing circumstances, what kind of activities caused it, how this made me feel etc. It was strange having to give honest answers when I generally tried to brush over the pain and especially how it made me feel, it was quite an emotional exercise.

I was pleasantly surprised when I was called in to meet the doctor, he was remarkably nice and engaging, speaking to me as a person not a problem as I've often experienced with consultants. He firstly wanted to know a little more about the history of my pain and then began to look at the various scan images of me on his pc. I was asked more questions relating to the nature of the pain, what made it better/worse, how frequent etc, and then he asked to examine me. Thankfully, this only involved me standing in front of him while he felt different areas of my back. As I hadn't thought I'd need an examination I hadn't dressed appropriately (nothing new there) and had to unzip a high waisted skirt for him to get to the correct areas.

When he did find the right place, I thought I'd fly through the ceiling! He pressed his thumb in so hard and kept it like that for what seemed ages but was probably only thirty seconds. After my squirming and trying to wriggle away from him (which he seemed to find mildly amusing) he asked me to sit back down and said, "I have some good news for you. Firstly, the scans show no evidence of the cancer returning and secondly, I can't find any nerve damage either." Now this was a revelation.

For nearly three years this had been the line I was told, 'probably nerve damage' usually followed up with, 'not a lot can be done.' So, to hear that this 'probably' wasn't the case was the best news I'd had in ages.

The doctor then went on to say that his diagnosis would be that I had a large knot of muscles in my back that was causing the pain. When I think back to the way I'd struggled with the surgery pain which had in turn caused my whole gait to become uneven this wasn't surprising. He then went on to describe to me the various ways I could deal with the pain including acupuncture, massage, trigger point massage, yoga and TENS machine.

I left his room feeling like I could walk on air I was so happy. Prior to this appointment I had been taking a high dose of painkillers and living with the fact my pain would probably never leave. Here I was walking away with some proactive measures that I could do myself to help ease and in turn maybe cure the pain, I couldn't stop smiling. Furthermore, he told me that exercise including running wouldn't have to be avoided if I made sure to take appropriate action afterwards whether by massage, TENS machine or anything which would help release the muscle tension.

The letter that I received following this appointment was also pleasing as it showed the consultant had listened to me; another shortcoming in specialists I'd met previously. He'd written in detail about me, my cancer, the treatment and his findings.

The suggestions he'd made about managing the pain were all listed; I'd already invested in a massage ball and a TENS machine. The latter was a revelation. To begin with it felt more like electric shock treatment. I placed the sticky pads around the areas of my lower back that felt most painful and switched on the small device attached by wires. I learnt through trial and error to check that the intensity was turned low before turning on or I'd nearly shoot through the roof. I'm sure it could be used as a weapon of torture. I'm still unsure of the benefits but can confirm that somehow or other it detracted the pain. My reasoning is that the niggling sensation it creates distracts you from the pain rather than easing it. Either way, it had a positive outcome.

The massage ball was less successful. The consultant had recommended getting a dog toy as they are cheaper and look similar. I bought a small hard ball with rounded spikes from a pet store and placed it between me and the back of my armchair. It was uncomfortable and painful and whenever I stood up, the dog took it!

What the consultant hadn't included in the letter were his comments about Gabapentin. When I'd explained the dose I'd been taking and the effect they'd had on me he proclaimed them to be 'The Devil's work!'

In conclusion, pain management had been a success. The TENS machine was distracting, the dog ball annoying but best of all, the consultant and his letter had restored my faith in specialist care.

CHAPTER 48 IT'S ALL WRITE

By October 2016, my running had become more consuming and I'd decided to train for half marathon distance. I'd continued writing my blog, but the entries became fewer and further between as there was less to report on.

I'd been asked a couple of times whether I'd considered turning my blog into a book. It was receiving a wide readership and I had regular messages via the site. Through writing my kidney cancer account and sharing it on Twitter I'd become acquainted with other kidney cancer patients and carers as well as charity members. When I sounded them out about the idea of a book they were unanimously supportive and encouraging.

The trouble was, I'd never written a book, I wouldn't know where to start. I did have a history of writing though, aged six I wrote a story in my school news book that went on to fill two exercise books and was subsequently bound and put in the school library. I'd continued to use writing to express and in some cases, hide my feelings. My diaries stretch back to my early teens and I have reams of poems and songs I'd written in younger days. This latest venture though wasn't just close to home, it revolved around it. It would include personal information, there would be people, places, specifically hospitals to name. I'd written the first part of my blog account retrospectively from notes I made at the time. I would need to bare all, even more than a hospital gown would.

I never actually lodged a complaint to the NHS although, I knew my doctor had written to my surgeon and the letter hadn't been appreciated. I'd felt at the time that complaining wasn't going to right the wrongs that had already taken place. My way of dealing with this had been to publish the blog, highlighting not only the disease but some of the failings in treatment and care. This had the desired effect of raising the profile of kidney cancer and reaching out to other patients who I'd been privileged to get to know as a result. Complaining wouldn't have made me feel better, writing about it did and subsequently seemed to help others.

When I made the decision to go ahead with a book Jay suggested I find a local writing group.

After some research I settled on Tamworth Writers as they met weekly in the town centre on a Wednesday afternoon. I was extremely nervous making my way there for the first time and had no idea what to expect. The group met in the Town Hall, a place I was familiar with as I'd helped stage a fashion show there a couple of years before. I followed one of the members through to the large meeting room where other writers were sat discussing the previous weeks topic around a large table. I introduced myself, explaining I was hoping to get help with writing a book and they welcomed me in to join them.

The last time I'd seen that table it was covered with clothes and the room filled with models and dressers. Now there were notepads and books, cups of tea and sandwiches, it was all very civilised. All present were women. Apart from one, I was the youngest there which made a change. I'd found increasingly that my peers in the fashion industry were considerably younger, inexperienced and shared little in common with me. Looking around this room I could see I'd learn a lot from these ladies, and they were probably trying to get the measure of me. Although I was nowhere near as extrovert as I'd once been, neither did I blend in easily.

I stayed for the duration of the meeting, enjoying listening to pieces that had been written on the previous week's topic; a theme was given weekly as a writing prompt for short stories or poetry, journaling or nonfiction. The following week would be Spider, this was perfect for me as that was my dogs' name. I left feeling accomplished even though I hadn't done anything, I'd attended. I'd plucked up the courage to go along and I'd joined in with discussion, even mentioning my ongoing book project. It was another new venture.

Yoga, running, cycling and now writing, the things cancer had led me to.

My elation at new beginnings was curtailed somewhat in late October when our beloved Spiderdog became suddenly very poorly. He was fourteen and so no spring chick in dog years but had always been a strong and active collie. An emergency trip to the vets confirmed the worst, he was not going to pull through and later that morning went to sleep peacefully. The vet was extremely kind, giving over the treatment room to us. He even allowed time for Jay to fetch Finn so they could be together as he left us. Watching his beautiful brown eyes close was heart wrenching, he was my friend and confident, companion through so much, a vital part of my routine and recovery. Being able to get back out and walk him had been a milestone, something I'd cherished and rejoiced in. Leaving him there I left a small part of my heart, he was irreplaceable.

CHAPTER 49 FAST FORWARD

I received a letter telling me my next appointment to see the consultant would be April 24th. It had occurred to me though, as my fourth cancerversary came and went that I hadn't had a scan date. When I phoned to check it out, I was told that the April date was a mistake and the consultant hadn't asked for me to be scanned until June and so my appointment would be moved back until the results were in

This was totally understandable and not an issue, I mean scans aren't something to look forward to anyway. Why then when I put down the phone did my tears come? I think it's the need to know that everything is ok.

Four years is good going and so close to that five-year goal that I didn't want it to drag on, I needed my reassurance at around the same time I have that anniversary. It's the time I can't avoid thinking about it, so it'd be good to get the scan and annual check-up over and done with.

I did, however have plenty to keep me occupied as not only had my own collection of lycra clothing grown, I'd begun making a range to sell.

Now in my second year of yoga I was a familiar face at my local class and had become good friends with Gemma, the teacher and owner of Midlands Yoga. We'd discussed the possibility of teaming up to sell a range of yoga gear, but it had taken me a long time to get my confidence back. It felt like a big deal to put my own designs out there again, so I began by making a couple of items for Gemma. She was the perfect model and showed off my designs perfectly. Not only was she attracting attention to my yoga leggings and tops, but she was soon drumming up custom. Within a few weeks I had orders from class members at her new purpose designed yoga studio.

This was an excellent start but, I hadn't really wanted to go back to making to order, I wanted to sell off the peg. Gemma, full of enthusiasm, had a rail put up in the studio and display shelving. I made a small number of items for the studio and we were in business. I worked out a commission percentage for Gemma and added some foam rollers to the stock as well as lycra running belts I'd ordered wholesale.

I hadn't bought in stock before and ended up buying far too many foam rollers, I had them stored all over the place. It had been a great idea at the time, brought on by my pain management experience. I'd seen that there was a rise in popularity of the roller, despite it's no pain, no gain reputation. I researched the best production costs and shipping from China and got a good deal on fifty rollers which I could sell at a competitive price compared to other online retailers. What I hadn't bargained on was that Aldi and Lidl wouldn't be far behind, even TKMaxx began selling them at a massively reduced price. (I still have a few rolling around the bottom of wardrobes!)

The running belts were a far easier sell. Such a simple idea and the price I bought them in from China was impossible to beat, even by making them myself. A simple lycra tube that you step into and sits snug around your waist or hips. Four openings in which to slide phone, wallet, gel bars and a hook inside for keys, it was genius and worked perfectly. The branded belt (which was identical to the one I found and probably came from the same factory) retailed at £24.99 and I could make a decent profit selling them for £10. The yoga studio sold a few and I listed them on my website and eBay, selling them to runners, gym members, cyclists even to store insulin or for dog walkers, they were a winner.

The problem with deviating again into activewear was that my hospital gown design was once more pushed back into the shadows. There simply weren't enough hours in the day and I wasn't sure how to move forward with it.

I got so involved with the activewear that I even arranged a photoshoot of my own, the first for a long time. Joey had a good friend, Ali who used to model but diversified into photography. They met at the hospital as Ali also trained as a nurse and Joey was her mentor. Ali was a superb photographer, benefitting from knowing both sides of the lens. I'd seen plenty of her photos and knew she'd be perfect to capture some images for me. Both of my girls had modelled for me in the past, in fact so had their friends including Joey's husband Tom and Ruby's fiancé Kevin. Joey was willing to model some yoga clothing, especially as it was Ali taking the photos. My friend Nicky said her daughter wouldn't mind modelling and sure enough Millie agreed, she had a great look, edgy and beautiful.

One of my fellow yoga students, Ian taught at the local boxing school and said it would be ok for us to use their gym as a location. It was the perfect place for an activewear shoot, not only the gym and equipment but the boxing ring. There was also an industrial looking yard with ladders and tyres out the back.

The photoshoot went extremely well and Ali managed to get stacks of excellent images to showcase my designs. I also really enjoyed getting involved again, I had a vision once more and it was working, it was fun.

I also took some photos of Gemma myself at the yoga studio to give a feel for the clothing in that environment; plus not many models could pull the poses Gemma could on a yoga mat!

Business was taking off again and orders were coming in, the rail needed replenishing and my sewing machine was hot. I had no time for cancer and its associations, I had work to do.

CHAPTER 50 TUNNEL OF LIGHT

May 2017 and I have yet another water infection. This was accompanied by a sensation that felt like a hot flush whenever I had a wee, as I was hurtling towards menopause, I presumed this was also par for the course. My abdominal pain had not disappeared although I managed it better with yoga, I'm sure there was an improvement. However, the latest water infection needed to be sorted so I book an appointment with my GP.

While I explained my symptoms I also told him that I'd increased my running training and had entered the ballot for the London Marathon. That event was in April 2018 and as a warm up I'd also entered Birmingham half marathon, my place for that was secured for 17th October 2017.

He just raised his eyebrows and fixed me with a look that said, 'Really?'

I went on to tell him about the yoga I was doing, now twice weekly. I explained that I'd rather face things head on, aches, pains and all than sit in a chair writhing around with a TENS machine attached. I was honest and said that there were times when the pain intensified if I overdid things, but I thought I generally had good judgement and the exercise was beneficial.

What I didn't say was that after attempting a headstand I'd felt as though my guts had tied themselves in a knot and were about to burst out! I had remained the right way up since then.

My GP wanted to examine me, something I hadn't expected. As he felt my tummy around my scar I nearly jumped off the bed, it was so sore. It wasn't something I would naturally do myself, so I was quite surprised at how painful it was. After the examination I was sent for thorough blood tests.

Returning a week later I was happy to hear the blood tests were ok, only one in the red and I'm not sure that was significant. I was therefore surprised that he'd booked a CT scan, but I trusted him implicitly and so agreed to it. I was sent away with antibiotics and within a couple of days they'd seen off the water infection.

The following week Jay and I went away for a break to the seaside taking Finny with us. We'd only been there a couple of days and were out walking along the seashore when my phone rang, it was my GP's secretary. He'd marked my scan as urgent and the appointment that had been given was the following week which he wasn't happy about, requesting it sooner.

"Do you think you could get to a scan in a couple of days?" Came the question.

"I'm away on holiday sorry, I hadn't expected it to be as soon. Next week's appointment will be fine." I assured her and so it was left. When my Doctor wants to pull strings, he doesn't mess about. There are people complaining about six week waits and more, but I've not had that issue when my GP is involved.

The following week I set off for the scan. I should've been on auto pilot the number of times I've driven to the hospital, but I still managed to make a wrong turn, my concentration was off kilter. On arrival it's normally easy to find my way to the scan reception, that day though I got lost in the corridors and had to ask for directions. Booking in is usually straight forward but I'd forgotten to fill the required questionnaire in beforehand. By this time, it was becoming evident I was far more nervous than I'd realised for this scan which I'd been quite blasé about.

The waiting room was busy and conversation centred on what you're allowed to wear into the scanner. There are always experts present who've had numerous scans and know procedure inside out even though it varies for everyone. I sat quietly and removed my necklace. It was as I removed my jacket that I was brought into the conversation when top expert began admiring my tattoos. This always makes me feel a little uneasy as all eyes are understandably then drawn to my artwork. The sleeve had been started before kidney cancer and was worked on by my friend and tattoo parlour owner, Netty. We'd discussed the artwork I required as it was all original. I wanted the girls and Jay represented along with other imagery that is close to my heart. The result is a combination of a fairy like figure in green surrounded by shamrocks which was Joey, a pink mouse which was what we'd always called Ruby and the letters JJ wound into a heart. Other art included the Prince symbol, a hummingbird and Mary, mother of God all set-in roses. Since kidney cancer I'd had a small kidney made up of leaves set into the starry sky that ran through my design – that way I still had two kidneys.

Thankfully, I was first to be called out, much to the surprise of those who'd been waiting longer and so I was spared a detailed run through of my colourful arm. It wasn't the scanner I was needed for though, I had to have the blood tests that made sure my kidney would cope with the contrast dye being fed through my veins. Despite nodding that I knew my way, I still managed to miss the haematology department and had to make yet another detour. More awkwardness ensued when I was called straight through for my blood tests ahead of a waiting room full of impatient patients. I was beginning to wonder whether my GP had rung ahead!

The usual dialogue took place between me and the phlebotomist, "Do you mind me going in here?" Points to my colourful arm. "Not if you can find a vein." *Clenches fist and crosses fingers.* My little mouse gets the brunt of the piercing as her ears are placed either side of the best vein.

Back in radiology I was directed to waiting room No.2 where I joined the previous panel of experts whose current topic of conversation was fluid intake. Some had jugs of water with instructions to drink a beaker every five minutes whilst others appeared a little left out. One lady thought it best to get a second opinion as to why she wasn't having to fill her bladder, 'because we're scanning your chest', does little to satisfy her need to be in the bladder gang.

I took a seat by a small table where my obligatory water was delivered with the news I would have at least forty-five minutes to wait for the blood test results. It was then I realised my other oversight, I had nothing to read. Phones had to be switched off and there were no magazines, it really would be a long wait.

One of the experts had been telling all assembled her medical history in a, 'quid pro quo' manner with little success and was now attempting to engage me. I conceded I wasn't a CT virgin and alluded to surgery. The C word had its usual effect and in no time at all my kidney was raised by lung, bowel and breast cancer patients. I felt as though I were part of a virtual game of Operation where Mrs Expert drew out those of us with diseased organs with heavy sighs and tuts.

A member of staff decided to put the tv on for us which I hoped would distract morbid conversation. It was tuned in to a consumer program dealing with cases of fraud, negligence and accidents which did nothing to lighten the mood. I managed to zone out listening to Gloria Hunniford long enough for the waiting room to almost clear taking with it Mrs Expert who mouthed, 'Hope you're ok' shaking her head as she left.

Mr Lung and Mr Bowel cancer had entered a debate about whose hospital was the biggest, Lung was under Leicester Royal and Bowel was North Staffs. They then wished they hadn't asked me as I trumped both with the University Hospital. Time was dragging and I really needed a wee and fidgeted about a little too much. This caused Mr Lung to ask was I ok; apparently I looked a little nervous. I assured him I was fine and prayed my pelvic floor could take the fluid overload a while longer.

Thank God I was next to be called. In some hospitals they canulate you before getting into the scan room, here they put the venflon canula in while you're on the scan bed. The guy piercing me was very gentle and helped put me at ease by chatting about my chosen outfit which I could've worn to a yoga class. He said I looked sporty which made me smile as I lay facing the all-seeing tunnel of light. Once the canular was in place it was business as usual, arms above head and I was left to be fed to the machine.

No matter how many times I've been in that situation it never gets easier. I passed under my name, hospital number and age illuminated above me into the white donut. Looking up lights flashed around the silver lining of the tunnel and an instruction read, 'Don't look into the laser' which you realise you're doing a little too late. Backwards and forwards a couple of times before being fed out once more and joined by a nurse to have the contrast dye fed through. As she left me again I hold my breath and breathe a couple more times whilst moving backwards and forwards under the beams before the nurse returns. All done.

I'm led to a cubicle next where the venflon is removed and I'm advised to sit back in waiting room N.2 for ten minutes before attempting to leave. When the nurse asks if I'm ok, I weirdly feel my tears coming and can only nod. This scan business really can mess with your head. She gives me a knowing look and leads me back to the waiting room.

Mr Lung is now discussing the hazards of travelling in an ambulance, Mr Bowel is agreeing saying he was rolled off a stretcher going along the A50. My ambulance experiences aren't required and I sit quietly before rising to go home.

After feeding the parking meter I sat in the car to eat my banana and flapjack, a ban on eating before the scan meant I was beginning to feel very faint. I had to keep my eyes down as patients arriving with nowhere to park were hovering around my car hoping I'd move off and leave them my space. Three hours after arriving I was back on the road home leaving behind the images of my abdomen and pelvis. Next, to hope and pray that the scan silver lining was reflected in my results.

CHAPTER 51 NO 1 FAN

Only three days after the scan my GP phoned me with the results, no evidence of disease. A huge sigh of relief followed. I think I may have mentioned before but, my GP really is the best!

That same week as I was stitching away listening to the radio my attention was grabbed by the subject matter. Doctors. I had taken to listening to a local Midlands station BBCWM, it was another lifestyle change that'd crept in over the previous few years. I couldn't put up with the generic man, woman DJ format, laughing at each other's jokes let alone the auto-tuned, clones that were churned out as popular music. I much preferred 'talky radio' and so flicked between Radio Four and BBCWM. The mid-morning show on WM could be informative and hilarious, I enjoyed listening to the Brummies' phoning in to moan, complain or tell their tales. As much as the subject matter being discussed, I could relate to these people and it reminded me of my Birmingham family. This morning the question was about GP practices and whether doctors were as caring anymore. There were numerous complaints about lengthy waits and dismissive doctors, there didn't seem to be any positives coming through. Well I couldn't have that. I left my machine and dialled the number for the station.

"I'd like to put forward a positive side to GP's."

I explained to the researcher the excellent service I received from my own doctor and I was asked to stay by my phone and I'd be called back shortly.

Five minutes later the phone rang and I was being put through to the presenter, live on air.

"You have a GP success story to tell?" He asked.

"Yes, my doctor is excellent, I couldn't ask for a better service." I go on to say briefly why I've had so many appointments in recent years and how efficient and proactive my doctor is.

"I think we'd all like to know who your GP is, where are you calling from?"

Well I hadn't expected this, but I obliged with which surgery I was at and my doctor's name, I felt like a member of his fan club.

By the time I came off the phone I realised that this would most probably get back to my doctor, at least I hadn't given my name. I had no plans to visit the surgery for a while. I was still suffering with pain around the area of my surgery wound but could rest easy knowing it was nothing sinister. I'd had issues with using my core strength during yoga, no matter how hard I tried, it didn't ever seem to improve. There was always the possibility that I was doing more harm than good partaking in some of the exercises, maybe I'd have to admit that this wasn't going to improve.

Thankfully running wasn't affected in any way. I continued training three times a week, the only time I felt pain was when I climbed hills but that didn't stop me going up.

The downside was having to reach for painkillers now and again. I wasn't tempted by those devilish Gabapentin and wouldn't consider touching tramadol but cocodamol were taking the edge off and despite feeling defeatist, I did take them off and on.

I was still in the process of putting my book together but got cold feet about a real-life depiction and had begun devising a fictionalised approach. This meant speaking to family and friends who would get a mention and asking them to create a new identity which was fun. We could all choose who we'd like to be.

Fictionalising place names, particularly hospitals was a tad more difficult so I put in the nick names used locally for the time being, with a note to ensure I changed them later.

Not much happened regarding my cancer story, not enough for me to be writing daily or even weekly. I continued with my running and business blogs but it was getting hard to keep up with everything. I'd gone from doing little to having way too much to stay on top of. I decided to merge the running blog with the unfashionable cancer one. After all, one did lead to the other. That's when I realised it was after all part of my story. What happened to me wasn't just the transition from fashion victim to cancer survivor, the road to survival was via my fitness pursuits. I decide to make this, particularly my marathon training, a bigger part of the picture.

In July, I finally got to have my appointment at the University Hospital which this time is with the specialist nurse, Clare. Whilst originally a bit put out that I wouldn't get to see the consultant again after that initial meeting, I was now extremely pleased I would get to see Clare and looked forward to another chat with her. The last appointment was excellent, she was so helpful, answering all my questions and reassuring me no end. We're almost the same age, a year apart and have the same birthday. Even better, she's also a runner – a particularly good one.

I've never needed a car of my own as I'm insured on Jay's and the girls as well as my Mom's Micra. It's the latter that I chose to drive to my appointment on that day and to take full advantage, I called in to do some shopping before I headed to Birmingham. While I was pushing my trolley around Morrisons I received a phone call from a withheld number, it was Clare, the kidney cancer nurse. Chirpy and friendly as I'd remembered her the call soon stopped me in my tracks.

"I thought to save you making the trip over we could have a quick phone chat instead."

"What? You don't want to see me?"

"It's not that", she faltered a little, "it's just that it's a long way to travel, I thought it would save time."

"I'm... I don't understand?" I faltered. "I thought you needed to see me; I've been waiting so long."

Clare quickly picked up how I was feeling but it was too late. She tried to interrupt but I continued.

"This appointment is so important to me, I don't care how far I have to travel, it means a lot to get to talk with you, face to face. I thought you understood?"

"I did, I do, honestly I'm not trying to put you off, come, you can still come over." The nurse backtracked but I knew. I knew I was surplus to requirements. Just another patient on the list. The long list that they were struggling to get through. Why should I take a place? A patient from another hospital, two other hospitals. A patient whose blood tests and scan had come back clear. Surely a quick chat; a reassuring word as I multitasked, health care and big shop all in one would suffice? Was this it, my third hospital trying to get rid of me before I even had an actual factual appointment?

"Don't worry, you can still come if you like," she reiterated.

If I like? "Do you know how many times I've been dismissed already?" I was getting annoyed. "If it's too much trouble then say so, if I'm not worth your time then tell me?"

I'd had enough of being fobbed off, feeling unworthy of treatment, even appointments now. Clare backtracked quickly.

"I've not put this across very well, I'm sorry. I really didn't know this meant so much to you, of course you can come and I look forward to seeing you very soon."

I paused. Was this the time to give in? Was my cancer really not that significant? Standing in the cereal aisle with tears rolling down my cheeks this had to be the worst cancer brush off so far but I had to stand my ground. I deserved to be seen, I had as much right to expert advice as the next cancer patient.

"Ok, I'll be with you in about forty minutes."

"Great, I'll come out to meet you, drive carefully."

I could still go home, cut my losses.

"Ok, thanks." Last chance.

The traffic was horrendous and there were diversions in place throughout the city centre, Birmingham was undergoing some huge changes, building and road works seem to surround every junction. My glasses started steaming up, I couldn't see with them or without them. The Micra unlike Jay's car only has five gears and aircon is via the window. This was not a day to be navigating gridlocked roads, the sun was beating down, it must have been at least 22 degrees, God knows what temperature the car had reached.

When I turned on the air vents I got covered in grit, I don't think my Mom must ever have used them. No air seemed to come in, the car felt like an oven and it was turned up high.

The University Hospital has a few different approaches, so I'd left my phone sat nav running for when I neared the hospital (the Micra isn't equipped with one of those either.) Unfortunately, as I turned off the A38 so did my phone, I glanced down to read, 'phone apps are shutting down due to overheating.' Brilliant.

The hospital loomed up ahead of me, the sun's rays illuminating its spherical outlines and then, like a mirage it vanished. I negotiated one mini roundabout after another, catching glimpses of the monster medical centre then losing sight straight after. Signs beckoning me towards my destination, I followed excitedly catching sight of a multistorey car park. Pulling up to the barrier I read, 'Staff Only.' Expletives hit the malfunctioning fan!

Taking a deep breath, I reversed back onto the never-ending hospital highway and continued circumnavigating Britain's biggest hospital. With twenty minutes to spare I managed to locate some patient parking near the old building which meant a lengthy trek over to the new centre where outpatients were held.

The beautiful weather had brought people out into the sunshine. The lawns in front of the main entrance resembled a park, people lay reading books, eating ice creams and chatting with family and friends. The difference here was the number held up by crutches, struggling with slings and laying on trolley beds with drips attached.

Once inside the huge entrance to the main building it was hard to know where to look, every which way – including upwards, was bustling with activity. I passed through the first reception area into the second to await my call to the third. Each seated waiting area is distinguished by its seat colour, I was sent to the blue chairs to watch scrolling screens that intermittently flashed up patients' names and instructions of where to go next. I looked around, all heads faced the screens, no one wanted to miss their turn. I'd planned on going through my notes for the nurse but found myself glued to the screen, I was still ten minutes early.

It was now that I felt alone. I'd insisted on going by myself, no point taking anyone else along, after all it was to discuss my results and ongoing care. Sitting in this huge hospital amongst so many other patients now made me feel quite lonely.

So, there I sat; in the blue section of the waiting area, blue seats, blue walls watching the screen roll over with patient's names. I checked my list, the time, the screen. I felt small and insignificant, part of me wanted to walk out of there and save them the effort. Then I saw my name splashed across the screen with an arrow directing me onwards. I made my way through to the final waiting room and had barely sat down when my name was called, bang on 2pm.

Clare came to meet me and smiling took my hand leading the way to a consultation room. She was lovely, exactly as I'd remembered her. The words of my daughter rang true in my head. After the upset earlier she'd spoken to me and said the call I'd received that morning was a mistake, the nurse had simply misread things and called it wrong. How could she possibly know what I'd been through previously, we'd barely had any time to talk at that first meeting with the consultant.

Reaching into my bag I took out my prepared notes, she was about to find out.

I spent almost an hour talking to Clare, she showed no signs of wanting to hurry my appointment and was extremely attentive. I had no reason to think my presence wasn't wanted there, maybe I was wrong. I felt a real connection with this nurse, I had from the moment I met her, maybe that's why it had hurt so much thinking I was being fobbed off. Before I left, we spoke about running and I told her about my forthcoming half marathon. Clare ran regularly and covered far more distance than I did, often getting in ten miles after work which was some major achievement. Her times were excellent too, I was impressed. I was relieved, she cared and it showed.

CHAPTER 52 ON MY MARKS

I'd managed to run the half marathon distance twice before the big day. Training had begun back in April so I had been attempting to run 13.1 miles for six months. My running nights were always Tuesday and Thursday when I'd cover between three to four miles each time. Jay ran with me although being much faster, he would double back at a set point and look out for me along the way. I was treating the shorter 5k distance as speed training, averaging around 8.40 minutes per mile, completing in around 26 minutes. At the weekend I'd focus on longer runs of five miles plus. On both occasions I'd run the 13.1-mile distance I completed in 2.03hrs which I was pleased about. My goal for the race day was to break the two hour barrier – a big ask!

To help with the more technical aspects of running longer distances I'd joined a local running group, who met a couple of times a week close to my home. I attended one session a week to put in a few extra miles as they generally ran around seven miles an evening. I only lasted about three months though as I found running and talking wasn't my style. I can appreciate why running clubs are so popular, particularly with female runners as there is safety in numbers, especially on dark winter nights. There is a camaraderie amongst runners as well, not only in clubs but online in virtual groups. I'd hooked up to UK Run Chat on Twitter where oodles of encouragement could be found whether training for a marathon or starting couch to 5k. However, the whole social aspect of running simply didn't hold any appeal to me, I already had a running partner in Jay and we had friends to socialise with. I'd imagined it would be like the athletics club I'd attended as a teenager where the focus was on the business of running. This however had a much broader appeal and wasn't the right fit for my needs.

Since taking up running in 2014 I'd learnt a lot about myself. I had far more stamina and motivation than I'd realised and I'd surprised myself with my competitive edge. Running had helped to focus my mind as well as improving general fitness which also benefitted from a better diet while training. Where I would dwell on worries and concerns about my health, I'd found a way to quieten my mind. When I ran, that was all there was to do; put one foot in front of the other and breathe. My body worked in synch with my mind, every organ and muscle keeping me going; how could there be anything wrong if I could run like that? Simply feeling my heart pound in my chest was reassuring. I was one step ahead.

I chose to raise funds for two charities close to my heart – and kidney. The first, Facing Up 2 Kidney Cancer was one I'd supported previously. All monies go directly to a kidney cancer project at University College Hospital, London. The second, Kidney Cancer Support Network is the patient led charity I'd been introduced to late last year.

I set up a Total Giving Page with the title, An Unfashionable Cancer Marathon; this would be the halfway mark.

I would turn fifty at the end of the year and March 2018 would mark five years since surgery. Back then I would never have contemplated running, let alone completing a marathon. By taking on these challenges I wanted to prove to myself and others fighting kidney cancer that there was still so much that could be achieved. I was aware that I was one of the lucky ones, recovery had granted me the ability to run. Cancer doesn't have to be the end of life as you know it, it can also be the beginning of so much more. I was living proof; yoga, writing, new business pursuits as well as marathon running.

My half marathon fundraising was going well, the £1000 target was getting closer; and so was the race. My social media presence was at a high, sharing training progress and fundraising links as well as the gear I'd be wearing on the day. I'd trained so hard for this and was going to tell as many people as possible.

On Sunday 15th October 2017 I would reach the halfway point of my Unfashionable Cancer Marathon adventure when I ran the Great Birmingham Run. I was determined to run every step of the way.

The week before race day I discovered a new ailment, Maranoia. I was terrified of getting ill or injuring myself before the big day and so virtually hibernated. I did risk attending my yoga class although I asked anyone with a cold to declare themselves and move to one side.

Apart from the obvious preparation, that six months of training I put in three times a week, there were other important factors that needed addressing. Top of the list what should I wear? I checked out the new prints at my favourite fabric supplier and after much deliberation chose the Hip Hop design, colourful, loud and with that hint of pop fashion I love.

I also needed a running vest, it had to be green; the colour of my chosen charity Kidney Cancer Support Network and Facing Up 2 Kidney Cancer and it needed printing. The charity names went on the back and it wouldn't have been complete without my business moniker on the front, MISSFIT!

Ruby sorted me out with some nice sparkly green gel nails which just left my hair but my maranoia was so bad I was on lock down and decided to wear a cap instead!

The morning of the race came around quickly and I was a bundle of nerves, it wasn't so much the run but getting there. I worried about traffic, parking, directions, getting in the right pen and the big one...needing a wee! Fortunately, we don't live far from Birmingham, so a short drive and we arrived with plenty of time, parked easily and got clear directions to the event. First stop was of course the portaloos and then we headed to the start point, Jay and Ruby were there as support (Joey had to work) so I had no baggage to sort.

The start was near the finish line where both the half and full marathon runners ended, the latter of which were coming through thick and fast at this point. The atmosphere was already exciting as those running the marathon were cheered across the line.

It wasn't long before I was parted from my family and had to find my way down to the Green Wave start point (after I'd found another portaloo.) I was relatively early so managed to get near the front. It was remarkably subdued as we waited, quite a bit of limbering up and sports watch checking but not much chatter.

The first two waves had their warm up and moved off and we were edged forward, unfortunately I'd chosen this moment to retie my laces and so dropped away from the front as people hurdled over me. When I spotted Jay and Ruby waving, I got so excited, all nerves disappeared as it was finally time to run. We had a short warm up which no one seemed to be paying any notice of before the countdown and we were away.

I can't describe how it felt to be running down past the Selfridge building and out towards Digbeth. Routes I trod regularly but usually with a trolley full of fabrics. The crowds at this point were amazing, loads of whistling, cheering, people calling out our names. As we headed out of the city towards the warehouses the crowds thinned and I really enjoyed passing through these familiar buildings whilst running in a huge pack, it was so strange.

I think there must have been points where I zoned out and was simply running, that happens to me often, I forget where I've been and wake up from my thoughts to realise I'm two miles down the road. When we headed into Cannon Hill Park I had a minor panic as I saw the sign for 8 miles and knew this was impossible. *I've joined the marathon route!* This thought flashed into my head so I had to ask another runner who laughed and explained that the signs are mixed around the course.

I soon realised that what I'd heard about the course having had hills removed that year was untrue. There were most definitely, 100% hills. The one we climbed up between mile 7 to 8 was a beast of a hill but I never once stopped. Since I began training I've always kept on running, no matter what. I feel that some bad luck will befall me if I stop so even if it's baby steps I run. If I must wait at a curb side I jog up and down. Let me tell you, by the time I got to the top of that hill I was seeing stars. I thought I'd need oxygen!

The other disappointment on the day was how congested it got. I was in the green wave and soon began meeting runners from the white wave. It wasn't long before we were in amongst the slower marathon runners and a few of the orange wave. At times it was so congested I was almost running on the spot so I didn't stop still. I found myself going up and down curbs a lot to avoid breaking pace.

I'll get my final moan out of the way, the bottles. Why oh why can't people take their own water to race events? I always run with water, mostly because having one kidney means I can't afford to dehydrate but also, it's easy. I understand that elite runners shouldn't have to run with bottles but for everyone else is it such a hardship? I have never seen so much waste! Not only were there nearly full bottles of water rolling underfoot but also gel packets making the road sticky in places. There must be a better more sustainable solution...oh yeah, carry your own water! The clean-up must have been phenomenal (and costly).

It was a huge relief to reach Bournville and turn, the support from the crowds there was great too, and we were heading downhill. By this time we were meeting more marathon runners and passing the last wave of half marathon runners on the opposite side of the road. I'd avoided high fiving anyone around the course after reading Running Like A Girl where it results in the author tripping up a curb and landing flat on her face in the London Marathon. Running back through Selly Oak I did managed to high five a pug though.

One of the bonuses of wearing something I'd made was the great promotion I was giving my business. So many people called out about my leggings and many runners complimented them as well which made me smile. It gave new meaning to 'running a business'!

Mile twelve came as a complete surprise as I think I must have zoned out again. The Pershore Road had been more congested coming back and as I hadn't set my Strava app going I had no idea what my pace was but knew it was slower than usual. By this stage I was feeling tired and the temptation to have a little walk was strongest. I kept on though, my legs were fine I was just a bit weary. Having never tried energy gels I'd carried six jelly babies in my running belt. I'd had one at miles three, six and eight and with a little over a mile to go had one more.

Turning the corner onto Bradford Street was a huge relief, I knew exactly how far was left, I'm a regular at Barry's Fabrics so it was a short stroll back past the Bull Ring and up Moor Street. Well, unless you've just run the best part of 13 miles! Never has 'that' hill seemed as steep. My last jelly baby needed to give me one hell of a sugar rush to climb it.

There was a complete mix of finishers making their way up the hill, many walked but more pushed on spurred by the fantastic crowds. By the time we turned onto Moor Street and could hear the announcements as runners passed the finish line I was feeling very emotional. I was reminded of my reasons for doing the run, the finish line was a big milestone for me.

Over the final few hundred yards I searched the crowds for my family, I knew they'd be there somewhere. I spotted Jay first and tried to get across to him but was blocked by a marathon finisher waving a huge glass of gin and tonic. Further on I heard Ruby calling and saw her as I crossed the line at 2 hours, 8 minutes and 21 seconds.

My tears came as I slowed down, I'd done it. I didn't feel too bad either, but the relief was huge and I was glad to get a big hug off my husband and daughter. I followed the line of runners collecting finisher bags and headed straight off back to the car. I did of course get my medal out and put it on, but I wanted to go home.

Would I do it again? Half marathon probably, but not a large event like Birmingham. It was an enjoyable day especially being able to run around my second hometown but just too big, I'd prefer smaller races.

I was immensely proud to be a Great Run Finisher though and as such wore my medal all that week, including shopping, yoga and writing group.

Training for the big one, 26.2 miles began almost immediately as well as the other important preparation, what to wear?

Proudly wearing my Half Marathon Finisher Medal at Midlands Yoga & Tamworth Writers

CHAPTER 53 SURPRISE

I knew it was a long shot when I applied for London Marathon, the ballot makes it notoriously difficult to get in. I'd heard of serious runners applying for a place over many years and still never succeeding. There were also quite a few first-time lucky applicants. It doesn't seem fair; there are the runners who are out there training, year in year out in all weathers, building up their mileage in preparation for London Marathon. Conversely, you have the complete novice who, after a few drinks with mates makes a one-off application to run London and gets accepted. This was a sore subject with members of the running club I'd joined briefly. There was one guy who'd run twelve marathons and applied seven times in a row, still no place for London, it was wrong. The only other way to get in was by running a Good for Age time; mine would have to be a sub four hour, they'd accept 3.55:45 and that really wasn't doable.

The way you get to find out is via the Marathon News, a publication produced by London Marathon which is sent by post. The front cover will either display an image captioned with the words, 'Congratulations, You're In!' or the more often, 'Sorry! You have been unsuccessful.'

As October crept closer I'd begun to change my mind. London seemed too far, too big, too overwhelming. My marathon attempt wasn't about the razzamatazz and fanfare, celebrities and media coverage, it was about my personal finish line. That could be wherever I wanted it to be and I really should have chosen a course more suitable to my ability. Not that London was a bad option, but it would be packed and after the experience of being penned in at Birmingham Half I should have known better. For Birmingham there had been approximately 9,000 marathon entrants and 12,000 half marathoners like me. London saw numbers in excess of 40,000 and that's not counting the crowds of onlookers and supporters. No thanks.

I heard the post drop through the letterbox and could see a magazine in its cellophane wrapping. Before I noticed the print, I could see the image of a runner, sitting on a pavement head down. Sorry, you have been unsuccessful in gaining a ballot place, it read. Don't worry, it went on, there are still plenty of charities looking for runners. I whooped with joy! What a feckin' relief. I hadn't realised the amount of pressure I'd put on myself, not only by training for a marathon but going for the big one. The travelling it would have involved for my family, associated cost, it was all unnecessary, I needed a straightforward marathon not a showcase event.

There were lots of other marathon locations listed in the magazine but none that appealed. Edinburgh seemed to be the one they really pushed above the rest and that was even further away. I wasn't a pin in the map kind of runner, this was personal. Another issue I had was with the charity place advertisements. I'd heard about these already, major organisations offering a place in big races, including London in return for large amounts of fundraising, often starting at £5,000. It somehow didn't seem ethical. Not that the charities weren't deserving but that it could mean running for a cause that meant nothing to you and putting yourself under immense pressure to beg the money from friends, relations and anyone willing to fund your place in a race.

The other problem I had with London concerned where the entrance fee went. It was £39 of which only a small percentage went to charities, most being spent on salaries and undisclosed running costs.

As relieved as I was, I still needed to find myself a place in another marathon race. I had to give my full marathon choice some considerable thought; not too big, not too far away, not too commercial, at the right time of year. I don't like running in the summer months as I get way too hot, springtime would be perfect. I needed it to be only about the run. I'd hovered over one location for a while, everything fitted the bill and there was another major plus point for me. The Shakespeare Marathon in Stratford on Avon has an entry limit of 4,000, it's run in May and organised by the Rotary Club who donate more than half the money raised to local charities. All of these ticked the box for me but the added extra was that, as a writer working on her first book, what better inspiration than to follow the bard himself. It was meant to be I signed up and stepped up my training ready for my first full marathon race on Sunday 13th May 2018.

Shakespeare Marathon wasn't the only milestone I was to cross imminently. On December 21st, 2017 I would be fifty years old. How to celebrate that had been the cause of much discussion but it was settled that we would have a meal with family as partying so close to Christmas was always problematic. Everyone is so busy, family visiting, works do's and Christmas preparations get in the way of arranging any other get together. I'd found over the years that it was easy to hijack Christmas celebrations as everyone's in the party mood at that time, so my birthdays were never dull.

As Jay's work wound down ready for the holiday festivities, he was asked to attend a work colleagues' engagement. It was still a couple of weeks before the Christmas break and so I agreed reluctantly to go along with him as it was only down the road at the local football club. The weather was awful, snow had fallen and turned to ice underfoot and it was bitterly cold. Jay advised I dress up so walking even the short route to the venue was hazardous in heels.

Arriving outside we hung back a minute as it didn't seem as though we had the right place. Lights were on but it was quiet and there was no-one about. Jay said we should poke our heads in the door and see what was happening, I just wanted to get out of the cold so swung open the door to, "HAPPY BIRTHDAY!"

As my eyes adjusted to the bright lights I began to recognise people, random faces smiling and laughing. A school friend of mine, Lorraine I'd not seen in years, a sister-in-law, my Mom and her neighbour, Laura and Thomas then as I saw more friends and family the penny dropped. A surprise party. For Me.

Jay followed me in smiling. I couldn't believe he'd managed to arrange this. He'd had help from the girls and family, but I hadn't had a clue. They had sorted a whole night's playlist of music I'd like and decorated the room with photos of me. There was a beautiful cake in the shape of a bee and a fabulous buffet. Tom had set up the sound system and lights, there was even a smoke machine. Best of all were the guests, some friends I hadn't seen for so long and others that had travelled miles to be there, braving the awful weather. Unfortunately, the blizzard conditions did keep a few people away but the turnout was wonderful and I felt so special.

Part way through the evening Jay took to the stage and made the most beautiful speech. He spoke about my Dad and how proud he would have been of me. My running pursuits were mentioned and Jay's own pride at my forthcoming marathon attempt. The words that brought my tears were of my cancer experience and how I'd fought back and overcome the obstacles it threw up. Telling of our fabulous weekend celebrating twenty-five years marriage Jay relayed the shock diagnosis that followed soon after and how far we'd come since that day. What better reason could there be to party, whatever the season we had overcome so much together.

CHAPTER 54 DESIGNED TO RUN

Marathon training was halted before it began as I started the New Year with remnants of a cold that had left me coughing uncontrollably. I coughed my way into 2018 and continued in this vein for four weeks before giving in to see my doctor.

The height of my concern was that I couldn't run. I had tried a couple of miles which left me hardly able to breathe and leaving anyone who saw me wheezing along the pavements in my running gear cancelling their New Year resolutions to keep fit.

After examining me my GP said my chest sounded ok and temperature was fine but to be on the safe side he'd send me for an X-Ray, more precautionary considering my cancer history. I was fine with this but the niggling 'what-ifs' that accompany any investigations of this kind never really leave. As I got ready to leave the room I couldn't resist mentioning.

"Were your ears burning a few weeks ago only I took part in a radio phone in about GP's?"

He grinned broadly, "It was you? I've been teased ever since."

I apologised and said, "I can't really give you a big hug so it was a way of saying thank you for everything you've done for me." I meant it wholeheartedly, without him I may not have even received the scans I was due let alone specialist appointments.

The following day I turned up at the local hospital for my dose of radiation, one shot and I was all done. Wearing the hospital gown rekindled my creative desire to get rid of those dreadful NHS robes in favour of the one I'd designed and still not got around to marketing.

I made a trip back to the local cancer centre to see if I could get feedback from patients who regularly wore hospital gowns. The comments boosted my confidence no end, they were unanimous in their praise for the design and encouraged me to get it into production. I left buoyed up with enthusiasm and booked an appointment to have my design registered with the Intellectual Property Office. In the meantime I canvassed opinion for a new business name as it would need to be a separate entity from my pop fashion work. The title I came up with was Coverstory Clothing, this would incorporate other items associated with hospital visits and wellbeing including chemo hats, hospital bags and post-surgery cushions. Having some time out from running hadn't brought me to a complete standstill as in early 2018, Coverstory Clothing went live and I began receiving my first hospital gown orders.

Not being able to run was incredibly frustrating when I had a marathon to train for. The only plus side to being 'on the bench' was that I had more time to write. After changing the format from journal to fictional novel I realised it wasn't working. Writing as someone else didn't have the same impact and so I decided to begin writing as myself again, it made more sense. However, I wanted to blend my cancer story in with the business I ran and my marathon pursuit, I needed to brand it, give it some imagery. There was only one person for the job, Justin Price. Justin had created my business branding and logo for Missfit back in 2006, since then he'd worked his artistic magic on a variety of projects reflecting my work to perfection. More recently I'd been in touch about a logo for Coverstory and he created a look that complimented my existing business perfectly whilst giving the new company an identity of its own. I explained the need to combine the fashion business, my marathon training and the cancer story to be used on my fundraising page. It could be shared on social media banners and blogs too, something visual that said exactly what I was all about, running, writing and fashion. Justin nailed it as usual. The image projected my message loud and clear with me front and centre in running gear; The wording An Unfashionable Cancer Marathon was in bold type with my name and a backdrop showing me working. There were some photoshoot designer images and other graphic wizardry Justin had created for my website blended in as well as the Missfit logo. All of this was coloured in the blue, white and silver that comprised my branding and over the top in large red random brushstrokes was the word, RUN. It said so much with little text. A snapshot of my life from fashion victim to cancer survivor. I loved it.

The only problem I had now was to get well enough to train, so much hung on this marathon. My cancer finish line, the fundraising target and my book, it had to have a happy ending.

As I hurtled towards the finish line, metaphorically speaking I was playing catch up in training. Jay had been running with me throughout, gradually building up the miles alongside me, well actually way ahead of me. The farther I ran the harder it got. I thought back to my athletics club days and remembered my coach telling me I was built for speed. Cross country had never interested me, long steady jogs across fields and down canal paths. Worst of all would be the communal shower you were expected to have afterwards, I'd do anything to get out of those long runs. What on earth was I doing pounding mile after mile of pavement? It was boring, repetitive and bloody hard work.

I'd never realised how many hills Tamworth had and they all seemed to go up! We'd start on a long slow incline, cross a steep bridge, climb another slow gradient, hill after hill with few going down. There were turning points on the routes that would determine how far we would be going. I'd watch Jay running up ahead of me and pray he'd turn downhill. *Go left, go left, go.... oh no!* Right, up another slow, steady hill, where Jay would turn back to me and say, 'You'll thank me for this when you're in that marathon.'

Saturday mornings were generally long run days, each week building on the last, miles clocking up and distance building.

With eight weeks to go I'd only clocked up to fourteen miles, my time out with a cough had set me way back, I wasn't sure I'd have done enough.

I kept on, one foot in front of the other, week in, week out in all weather. Mostly we ran in the evening, as the mileage was rising, there wasn't time each morning before work to run much further than four miles. There was still an awful lot of running to do and time was running out.

CHAPTER 55 THE FINAL COUNTDOWN

If I compared my diary of six years previous with the one I sat writing in 2018, there would be a huge contrast. Both would be busy and leave little room each week, but the content bore no similarity. In May 2012 I'd been working on a variety of projects including helping to organise a summer fashion show and designing outfits for a local carnival celebration. As well as my day-to-day business, I was involved in all manner of fashion related pursuits which revolved around a diverse and often eccentric community of people.

March had always been a busy month with birthdays and anniversaries and that year Jay and I celebrated thirty years of marriage. There was also another forthcoming wedding, Ruby and Kevin were due to tie the knot in August, so I had the small matter of another wedding dress and four bridesmaids' gowns to design and create. Joey and Thomas had their own special calendar date approaching too, our first grandchild was due in early May.

Of course, sitting amongst those dates was March 13th, my five-year cancerversary. Although it was the date of discovery it wouldn't be until the day of my marathon when I would cross my final finish line and see cancer off once and for all.

April had two looming dates approaching. The first was my fifth annual CT scan at the University Hospital and three days after that on April 13th I would be running my first marathon.

I was so close to the winning post which metaphorically speaking would be the cancer free declaration. I'd wanted the finish line to coincide with running 26.2 miles, to hold my arms aloft and yell, 'It's over.' Unfortunately, however, as scans and appointments were now behind schedule, I wouldn't get this finality for a few more weeks.

I'd begun tapering down marathon training after reaching eighteen miles, the furthest I'd run. After losing time due to my cough and cold, I hadn't managed to complete a full marathon which was worrying. I had however, worked so hard for so long I was determined to complete the race, even if it was on my hands and knees.

Tapering had reminded me of the time when I enjoyed running. Being able to take on a steady five miles was wonderful; I could breathe again, enjoy my surroundings. The pace of life slowed as the miles decreased. Long runs were draining; they sapped my energy and enthusiasm for running. Now they were over, I had time for other things when I got in from a run, not simply collapsing in a heap.

One major worry was the weather, it was hotting up. Even after five miles I was overheating and the forecast for marathon weekend was pure sunshine.

My change in diet since going long distance had altered my shape. Always having a boyish figure, no lumps or bumps, now I was even more svelte and toned although conversely, I weighed almost a stone extra, apparently all muscle! My thighs and calves were very defined, I looked like a real runner.

When I arrived for my scan at the University Hospital, I was told that as I'd had a CT quite recently, I would be given a renal ultrasound instead. This was fine by me and I took my place on the scan bed while a radiologist introduced me to a trainee who would help do my scan.

Their chatter put me at ease and when questioned about general health I mentioned the marathon I'd be running in less than a week. The radiologist was also a runner and we chatted about training and predicted times. When I got up to leave I said, "I'd hoped to be able to cross the finish line knowing I'd seen the last of kidney cancer."

With his practiced poker face the reply came.

"I'm pretty sure that's doable."

That was good enough for me.

Fundraising had been going well despite my reluctance to push it too much. The whole concept of asking for sponsorship didn't come easy, never has. It felt too much like begging, holding out a hand for money; even though it was for a good cause. I'm amazed at the vast sums of money drummed up by individuals for charitable causes from a range of activities. Initial response to my plea had been wonderful with friends and family leading the way. As time went on, I'd relied upon sharing blog posts and training images alongside the Total Giving page. I managed to reach a wide audience which included other kidney cancer patients via the charity Facebook page.

One guy interested in my marathon attempt was John Thompson who had recently been diagnosed with kidney cancer. He was a keen runner and had contacted me with questions about my return to fitness, in particular; how long before I was able to run. I explained that running was a new pursuit post kidney cancer but gave him as much information regarding my road to fitness as possible. In return, he sponsored me £26.20 – a pound for every step of the way! Along with Judi Bond my other mono-kidney running pal, he continued to give sound advice regarding marathon prep. I was learning about hydration tablets and energy gels, for this race jelly babies weren't going to be enough.

I made the decision to contact the local paper the week before my marathon to raise publicity about my venture and hopefully boost fundraising. As a fashionista I'd regularly been snapped in varying poses usually involving holding garments, standing alongside models (never a favourite) or candidly at events. When the photographer for the paper arrived he had some questionable ideas about how I should be pictured.

I'd agreed to wear my custom-made leggings and charity printed vest but when he asked, "Shall we go over to the park and get you running?" I froze.

"Can't you just take some out in the garden?" I pleaded.

Finn had been barking angrily since the photographers' arrival and was staring menacingly at him from the back yard.

"I think we'll get some better action shots out in the open." He smiled, glancing over his shoulder at our terrier who looked ready to tear him apart.

Action shots?

With a reluctant sigh I began lacing up my trainers.

"Are those the ones you're wearing for the race?" Came the question.

"Yes," I replied hesitantly.

"Let's get some photos of them up close, say framing your face?"

What?

Exactly what I'd wanted to avoid was happening. You know those pictures in local rags where residents are angry at a road closure and told to stand by a street sign looking annoyed or sad? Or kids pass exams and are asked to jump for joy? Staged, fake photos that tell a story in clumsy, clichéd images. Well here I was, holding my trainers at jaunty angles either side of my grinning face. As for the park, I'm instructed,

"Run towards me. Run away. And back." by the photographer Who's secretly laughing inside while I race back and forth like a dog after a stick. As if that wasn't embarrassing enough, these photos would be distributed across the town in a few days' time.

Marathon task ahead for Debbie

Other preparation for the big day included getting in touch with the organisers of Shakespeare Marathon who suggested giving me a 'Shout Out' at the start of the race. I really was a glutton for punishment.

Reminding myself it was all for a good cause I checked into my Total Giving account a few days prior to the race and saw that it stood at a poignant £1,300.00. It was 13/03/2013 when my cancer story began and the marathon was being run on the 13th. Maybe my luck was changing?

CHAPTER 56 MY UNFASHIONABLE CANCER MARATHON

It's 8.57 on 13th May 2018. I'm amongst around 2000 runners waiting for the countdown to Shakespeare Marathon in Stratford on Avon. Alongside me on the other side of the railings are Jay, Ruby and Kevin, more excited I think than I am.

I'm wearing the same gear I had on for the Birmingham Half Marathon seven months ago. A green vest printed on the back with the charities I'm running for and on the front Missfit, my business and social media name. I've opted for the attention-grabbing Hip-Hop leggings again, may as well see if I can drum up any business orders along the route. The race number 1018 is attached to the front of my vest top with race clips that read 'Run Like You Stole Something' and my Asics trainers have a colourful graffiti pattern, I guess I'm quite noticeable. Normally I run in a cap, but I've opted to wear sunglasses and hope the sun doesn't make too strong an appearance or I'll overheat. The most important piece of kit I have on is my Garmin watch to help pace myself.

During training my pace has increased the further I've run. Previously I set an average time of 8.30 minutes per mile when running shorter distances. I'd ambitiously set out to run a marathon pace of 9.30 minutes per mile, what a fool I was. The seconds ticked over into minutes the longer I ran until I hoped for a marathon pace of around 10.20. The bib number 1018 gave me hope that I may match that on race day.

As we wait in Stratford town centre, I'm approached by a man who holds out his hand and tells me what an inspiration I am, he's read the local news story about my marathon attempt. All around me are runners wearing charity vests. MacMillan was often the most represented with Cancer UK always having a good show. Today it seemed that Mind, the mental health charity came out tops, probably to coincide with mental health awareness week. Next to me is an extremely nervous young lady, it's her first attempt at a half marathon, both full and half start the course together with full doing a second lap. She's envious of my support team who are encouraging me as we wait for the klaxon.

The guy starting the race is Steve Edwards, world record marathoner running his 822nd marathon this will be his 22nd Shakespeare Marathon the first having been in 1985. The start rope is lowered and we begin to move forward, slowly at first then momentum gathers. We cross the timing mat at the start line and the small chip attached to everyone's trainers is activated, the race has begun. Some of us will be running for a little over an hour others for more than six hours. The two distances each have a different coloured bib. For the marathon mine is red, most around me seem to be white for the half.

For the first part of the run we skirt around the town centre where support from spectators is excellent. Stratford on Avon is the most picturesque town I've run through, but my focus is on getting into a steady pace. Negotiating bends and keeping away from the barriers takes concentration with so many runners surrounding me, I have a dread of tripping over and ending my race at the beginning. I'd been positioned relatively near the front of the crowd at the start which meant I was being passed by more experienced and/or energetic starters. Avoiding feet and elbows was tricky until the road widened and we ran out into more suburban streets then out for a short stretch on the Evesham Road.

By this time, the field was evening out more. We reached the first drinks station just after mile two, but I was fine with my own water bottle. For this race I added an electrolyte tablet as recommended by John and Judi to aid hydration and in a running belt I also carried two energy gels and some jelly babies – to keep me company. I don't normally run with my phone but carried it so that I had contact with Jay – just in case. For the next couple of miles we wound around country lanes and then started to ascend to the village of Luddington. My hill training paid off as this barely challenged me. There was already a queue waiting for the loo at the first WC station just before the four-mile marker, thankfully that urge wasn't on me, yet. We ran through more country lanes and past houses whose occupants made the special effort to stand out and cheer us on. Kids holding bowls of jelly babies and motivational music along the route are always welcome together with the shouts of encouragement and there was no shortage here. My favourite resident was the guy spraying passing runners with a hose pipe, I was straight through that no messing.

By now runners had begun to settle into their pace and small groups were forming. I'd run past a couple of people only to be overtaken by them a little further on. Faces and charity vests became familiar as well as running styles. Quite a few runners were 'jeffing' by now, the run/walk method so called as it was taught by Jeff Galloway as a way to increase distance and endurance. I was overtaken by a guy dressed in full Shakespeare costume who must have been sweltering as the heat was really turning up by mid-morning. Then I heard an odd squeaking noise approaching and turned to see a man carrying what appeared to be a large backpack heading past me. As he moved in front, I could see it was a huge rubber boob complete with nipple, two handprints and the slogan Cop-A-Feel, a breast cancer charity. I ran behind the squeaky boob for about four miles.

As we neared mile eight the hill appeared. I'd heard about Rumer Hill and so Jay had surprised me a couple of weeks before the race with a drive over to familiarise me with the course and hopefully allay some of my fears. Facing it on foot was another thing entirely but I kept running, reaching the brow was a real achievement. Not long after this, on the first lap we turned off and headed back picking up the Greenway near to mile ten which is a gritty surfaced trail along a disused railway line. The track had a slight incline and by this time the sun, which had hovered around all morning decided to come out and play fully. For me this was the toughest part so far, there was hardly any shelter from the sun's rays and the incline was taking its toll. The worst part was knowing that shortly before mile twelve we would split from the half marathon runners and it would be game on for the big one. If the first 11.9 miles was not completed in two hours twenty-five minutes, runners would be directed to the half marathon course. I passed this point at around two hours and five minutes, just twenty minutes to spare.

We crossed an old iron bridge spanning the Avon before reaching another drinks station and portaloo point at the divide. The most welcome sight here were volunteers handing out wet sponges from a large barrel. It had dawned on me earlier as the sun beat down that I'd forgotten sun lotion and I could feel myself slowly frying. As we parted from the half marathon distance and headed past mile twelve, I felt like crying. It was the realisation I had it all to do again and more.

Curving around back out onto the main road I knew I could take it easier as I'd reached the marathon stage before cut off. It wasn't long before I stopped to take a walk and text Jay to let him know I was on lap two. He'd hoped to see me at the halfway point, so I'd presumed he'd not made it on time. It turned out he'd been directed to the wrong place and saw only the half marathoner's heading back.

I checked my Garmin as we reached the halfway point 13.1 miles, my personal best had been 2hrs 8 minutes and I was falling behind this by over five minutes. I heard a couple of runners behind me discussing how it had taken us longer to reach this stage than it had for Paula Radcliffe to complete a full marathon. The thought of running the entire course again was now beginning to fill me with dread. The sun was getting stronger and shade we'd enjoyed earlier now all but gone. Approaching 14 miles we were leaving the town behind for the second time and heading out on country roads.

It was now easy to see that more than half the field of runners had opted for the half marathon. Those of us still going were spread out along the undulating roads, at some bends I felt as though I was running alone. Climbing the hill at Luddington again was tough, I'd taken to Jeffing myself by this time and hills were a definite walk pace. I also nipped into the portaloo, no queues now, not even another runner in sight. On we ran through picturesque villages, past pubs which were by now filling up with lunchtime customers who cheered us on. When the 18-mile marker appeared, I knew what would be next, Rumer Hill part two. This time I don't think I could've run had I wanted to; my legs were beginning to feel painful. I couldn't even trot down the hill as my toes were also feeling sore. I took advantage of my more leisurely pace this time to stop and take a photo from the top of the hill, it was a beautiful view.

This time around we kept straight on taking a longer route through Long Marston and down to join Greenway South. The 20-mile marker felt surprisingly good as I told myself it was only a 10k run to the finish, 10k would be easy, I run it often, just not after 20 miles! What I didn't anticipate was the ferocity of the sun by this time. I'd already topped my water bottle up once and by mile 21 had to stop to refill it again. There were very few running now, I think we were all Jeffing. Passing each other back and forth. I'd set my sights on a woman called Hannah who had passed me earlier and I was determined not to let her out of my sight, but as she edged from my view I knew I was fading.

Mile 22 was my wall. I'd text Jay to let him know how far I'd got and tried to remain positive, but I felt beaten. Although there was only a little over four miles to go it felt an impossible task. The gravel pathway seemed to keep rising along the horizon and there was little shelter from the sun. I could feel my shoulders sizzling and my head was aching. As for my legs, they didn't even feel as though they belonged to me. At mile 23 there came relief by way of another bucket of sponges, cold water down the back of my neck gave me a boost and I pushed on. I took a photo of the mile 24 marker and sent it to Jay so he would know I was nearing the finish line. Normally the remaining distance would take me around 15 minutes but with my pace dropping to a staggering (literally) 11-minute mile it was going to drag. Along this last stretch was the official race photographer who called for me to look across and smile. Surprisingly, I look remarkably fresh in the resulting photo, probably wasn't pushing hard enough.

The final stretch took us off the Greenway and back along a road before a sharp turn down a small track that led to the recreation ground and finish line. I managed to maintain a steady jog now, every muscle in my legs ached and my toes were very sore, but I wanted to run to the end. As the main field came into sight so did Jay who, after shouting encouragement while I plodded towards him then ran alongside me till we reached the final stretch. I was on my own running down to the finish, my name was announced and I was praised on my choice of leggings. Crossing that finish line was incredibly emotional. I'd imagined it over and over, from first applying through training and along the route that day. The finish line was hugely significant marking five years since my cancer diagnosis. Ruby and Kevin held up a banner alongside Jay as I crossed the line. The medal was hung around my neck and I collected some water and a much-needed banana.

My tears came as soon as I met my family. It was such a huge achievement. I'd proved that a cancer diagnosis wouldn't hold me back in any way. In fact, I'd achieved far more in the past five years and was probably fitter now than ever. As for my time, 5 hours 15 minutes and 52 seconds. A way off my predicted 4.30-5 hours but a result I'm extremely proud of. Things I learnt from running a marathon; there's nothing wrong with jeffing, respect those hills, don't forget your sun cream, carry business cards and most important, it's tougher than you think. I said that this would be my one and only marathon and I stick to that statement. Many people have told me I'll change my mind but I'm very sure I won't. Long distance running is not for me. I ran a marathon for a specific reason, I trained thoroughly and ran it to the best of my ability.

I am now a marathon runner and a cancer survivor.

FINISH
MISSFIT
SHAKESPEARE MARATHON
1018

CHAPTER 57 FINISH LINE

It took about a week for the reality to sink in. I was a marathon runner. The final amount raised was £1,542 and every penny would be going towards kidney cancer research and patient care.

I'd crossed the finish line but had one more appointment to attend and one last box to tick. I was to return to the University Hospital a month later to meet my kidney cancer nurse specialist, Clare. I travelled over by train; Jay was driving straight from work and meeting me at the hospital.

Despite having completed the 26.2-mile run, I wasn't filled with confidence about my results. I'd had another water infection soon after the marathon; not surprising given how dehydrated I must have become. Then I had a routine cervical cancer screening which led to another referral due to 'suspicious bleeding.' Would these intimate investigations never end?

I'd been sent for a scan of my bladder and ovaries a couple of weeks after the annual renal and chest one. I wasn't feeling particularly well and was given antibiotics which led to dizzy spells. God knows how I ran that race!

The train ride over to the hospital gave me plenty of time to gather my thoughts which weren't exactly positive. Whether from the exertion of marathon training or the worry of so much poking and prodding, I was feeling quite down. I'm not prone to any form of depression; I'm more likely to suffer low confidence than mood. It's a good job because at no stage from diagnosis, through treatment to recovery was it once suggested or was I ever offered any form of counselling by the hospitals I'd attended, six in all.

For the most part I'd remained optimistic, stoic was the word used by my friend Laura back at the beginning of my saga. I suppose my true feelings came out in my writing; it was easier to express myself on a page. Now as my story neared its conclusion, I needed a happy ending.

It was a pleasant June day as I walked the path from the station to the huge glass fronted entrance. People swarmed in and out of the open plan foyer. Taxis came and went, their drivers darting about in search of passengers. The fruit and veg stall to one side made brisk trade as visiting friends and relatives bagged grapes and bananas. Alongside, patients of varying ages and abilities struggled to find a quiet place to smoke a crafty fag. I found a seat amongst this melee, as one amongst so many for whom this day could be life changing. All different but wanting the same; to leave this place with good news.

My phone rang. Jay had been stuck in traffic and although now inside the network of hospital roads, he was struggling to find parking. I attempted to guide him towards the multi-storey nearest the outpatient's department and with five minutes to spare, he appeared from the car park stairwell.

Familiar with procedure now, I booked in and we were moved efficiently from one waiting room to another before being greeted by Clare who hugged me warmly before ushering us through to a private room.

I'd emailed Clare in advance to tell her I'd completed my marathon as she'd been so encouraging at our last meeting, giving me a few running tips. We got chatting straight away about running and I proudly brought out both half and full marathon medals to show her. In return, Clare gave me an envelope with a contribution to my fundraising, I was quite overwhelmed.

She asked how I was filling my time post training and I explained that I was knee deep in bridal wear for Ruby's wedding. Amazingly, we discovered another coincidence as Clare had been a dressmaker in the past, making Holy Communion dresses! Born on the same day, dressmaking runners, the similarities kept coming.

It was time to discuss the most important business, results. Clare got the scan report up on her screen and read those beautiful words, no evidence of disease. She went on to say that my remaining kidney was a good size and the left renal bed showed no evidence of metastasis. The relief that flooded me was immense. My tears were falling before she finished reading. I had held so much worry and tension inside and it began draining away as the news sunk in. I felt somehow, I'd cheated and would be found out; I'd convinced myself the cancer would catch me again.

Better still, I was then told I could be signed off from consultant care and return to GP monitoring. However, should I have any concerns in future I would be able to contact Clare. Because of my complicated hospital history, Clare checked that I would be happy with this arrangement and I confirmed it was exactly what I wanted now. It was time to say goodbye. First though, more blood tests as my kidney function hadn't been checked for twelve months. Clare walked us out to the waiting room and gave me a final hug. It had taken nearly four years for me to get to see a specialist nurse. Central didn't have one and I wasn't at the District Hospital long enough to find out. It had been worth the wait to meet such a dedicated and sincere professional.

The blood tests were straightforward and we were soon on our way home. I kept repeating the same thing, 'It's over.' I couldn't wait to phone the girls and my Mom with the news. Jay took me for a meal later to celebrate and I went through my contacts texting everyone my wonderful results.

Life soon went back to normal, the new normal. My activewear designs were selling well and the design rights for my hospital gown had been approved. The book was taking a lot longer to get down; re-writing each blog post was like reopening a wound. I pushed it away several times and were it not for the encouragement of family and friends as well as my writing group and those kidney cancer patients I'd been fortunate to hook up with, it may never have been completed.

I haven't experienced the closure I expected to feel following cancer, it's a little like grief. It took a small part of me away and left me questioning what might have been.

In my case, I had a successful fashion business, would it have continued to grow? Did cancer take my confidence as well as my kidney? Was it something I ate? Did I drink too much? Is it hereditary? Oh, and the big one, will it come back?

So many questions remain.

What I do know is that on completing my story I'm now a marathon runner, a yogi and I've added swimming and cycling to my fitness regime. I've set up a new business with my hospital gown design which has attracted wonderful media attention and I've refocused my existing company on sustainable clothing. Not to forget I'm also an author.

When I started my blog, I'd had a rude awakening. One day changed my life forever. As far as making the best of an awful experience, I don't think I've done too badly.

I'm not planning on writing a sequel!

ACKNOWLEDGEMENTS

There are so many people to whom I owe a debt of gratitude for their love and support throughout my cancer adventure. Apologies to anyone not mentioned, I'd have to start another chapter.

Rose Woodward, James Whale, Malcolm Packer, Lee Dowding, Dr Steve Davies, Susan S, Judi Bond, Lisanne Vos, Jon Birchall, Sarah Pym, John Thompson, Justin Price conceptual designer extraordinaire, Laura and Thomas McCormick, Fi Lewis, Pauline Winch, Simona Stankovska and The Cavernoma Society, Gemma Beesley and the Midlands Yoga Family, Netty B, Claire Wright, Nicky Matthews, Jennifer Banks (the teeshirt still fits) Tamworth Writers in particular Patricia Pitt and Wanda Pierpoint for their editing expertise, Sharon Fox, Paula Da-Silva and the Tamworth Wellbeing & Cancer Support Centre, The Tamworth Herald, The Peel Runners, UKRunchat, Shakespeare Marathon and Muriel, Betty and Clara.

Websites for the charities that I've turned to for help can be found here
Kidney Cancer Support Network www.kcsn.org.uk
Kidney Cancer Uk www.kcuc.org.uk
Facing Up 2 Kidney Cancer www.facingup2kidneycancer.org.uk
Macmillan Cancer Support www.macmillan.org.uk
Tamworth Wellbeing and Cancer Centre www.tamworth-wellbeing-cancer-support.com
The Cavernoma Society www.cavernomasociety.org.uk

Special Thanks to Justin Price, graphic designer, ideas man and splendid friend who has put my words and thoughts into beautiful images time and time again. More of his incredible artwork can be found at www.justinrobertprice.com

The Tamworth Writers have a blog on which links to their various publications can be found here www.tamworthwriters.wordpress.com

For more on how yoga can benefit you, take a look at Midlands Yoga website.www.midlandsyoga.com

EPILOGUE

My finish line was to run a marathon, that would complete the book and hopefully put a full stop after cancer. It also saw the end of my love affair with running which became a chore; marathon training was intense and gruelling. Other runners said that after my race I'd get the marathon bug and book myself into another, not the case. A couple of weeks off became months and apart from a few 5K bursts, my trainers were back on the shelf.

As I write, I've been out for a few short runs for the first time in two years – no more marathons!

I continued to work on my hospital gown, applying for design rights and setting up a dedicated web shop for the Coverstory Dignity Gown. The start of 2019 looked promising as sales were boosted by an online campaign, Down With The Gown highlighting the lack of dignity given by standard NHS gowns. My involvement in this resulted in radio interviews and large social media interest, which in turn brought more sales. In March 2019 this was halted by the Covid-19 pandemic and the shortage of hospital scrubs.

Usually the uniform of theatre staff, the pyjama like two piece that comprised scrubs was now essential for the range of NHS staff coming into contact with the Covid virus. Hearing first-hand about depleting stocks, I joined the army of people sewing across the UK and became a Scrubber. Helping to set up a dedicated group in my hometown I continued making scrubs for three months, sending them into the hospital where my daughter worked and to my GP surgery. I had found a small way to show my gratitude.

A return to the all-seeing scanner came in August 2019 when, following headaches and balance problems I was sent for a CT which uncovered a brain lesion. This has since been diagnosed as a Cavernoma which had haemorrhaged. Baffled by medical jargon and frustrated with the lack of specialist communication I was rescued again by a Google search that led me to the dedicated charities that support Cavernoma sufferers., The Cavernoma Society and Cavernoma Alliance. Once again, my excellent GP stepped in to make sure I received the best possible care.

Things I wish had been available on diagnosis of kidney cancer;

NHS booklet about kidney cancer; I was only handed one of these three years later at my third hospital.

Information about the dedicated charity organisations offering support; Google introduced them a few weeks after my discharge.

Physiotherapy following surgery. What I received in hospital was a test to see if I could walk out of the place. Patients need advice about exercise moving forward, ways to prevent falling into bad habits and to correct posture during recovery.

Dietary advice related to my condition. I had 101 questions and Google threw out 1001 answers! A brief outline on food to avoid as well as recipes to ensure maintaining good health would be helpful.

Access to counselling. For some patients the return home following hospitalisation or on discharge from care can be daunting, especially for those living alone.

I made sure there is no mention of a journey in my book. That word has been eliminated as it suggests a beginning and an end. Cancer is a never-ending story that leaves you with far more questions than answers and although they can remove it from your body, it's harder to wipe from your memory.

A sequel was never planned, by that of course I refer to the chances of kidney cancer returning. The dietary changes, additional exercise and general strive for fitness I've written about were all to ensure I was in the best possible shape to fight any recurrence of the disease. Despite taking a vital organ, my recovery from cancer has taken me on an adventure, introducing me to new pursuits and wonderful people and I am grateful for each and every one.

ABOUT THE AUTHOR

Thank you for purchasing my book.
If you want to find out more about my business Missfit Creations, the Coverstory hospital dignity gown or connect on social media, please follow the links below or go to www.missfitcreations.com

Twitter @missfitcreates
Instagram @missfitcreates
Facebook @missfitcreates
Pinterest @missfitcreates
Linkedin @missfitcreations

Printed in Great Britain
by Amazon